NEW
UPHOLSTERY

NEW
UPHOLSTERY

DIANE WALLIS

SMITHMARK

This edition published in 1998 by SMITHMARK Publishers,
a division of U.S. Media Holdings Inc., 115 West 18th Street,
New York, NY 10011.

SMITHMARK books are available for bulk purchase for sales promotion and premium
use. For details write or call the manager of special sales, SMITHMARK Publishers,
115 West 18th Street, NY 10011.

Produced by The Watermark Press, Sydney, Australia.
Designers: Clare Forte and Cathy Campbell
ISBN 0-7651-0834-8
Printed by Skiva Printing, Hong Kong
10 9 8 7 6 5 4 3 2 1

Library of Congress Cataloging-in-Publication Data:

    Wallis, Diane.
        New upholstery/Diane Wallis. -- 1st Smithmark ed.
           p. cm.
        Includes bibliographical references and index.
        ISBN 0-7651-0834-8 (alk. paper)
        1. Upholstery. 2. Upholstered furniture. I. Title.
    TT198.W35 1998
    645'. 4--dc21   98-3897
                                            CIP

CONTENTS

INTRODUCTION

Upholstery takes the hard edge off the furniture and fittings we sit on, lie on, gaze at and lean against. It gives the bare bones of structure, the padded, fleshy resilience that invites us to sidle up and get comfortable. The outer covering may even have the jewel-like allure of a peacock's plumage. In short, it's an outfit; a fabulous fashion statement for furniture.

Upholstery probably has a lot more to do with decadence than purity of intention, form and content, and that's why it attracts me.

In the near past, upholstery has explored the depths of dreariness with utility taking precedence over beauty. Go back further in time and you will find that upholstered furniture, although a fairly rare commodity, was often sumptuous in the extreme. Today, the upholstery world is again brimming with some wonderful excesses in contour, color and trim which gladden the heart. This is surely the essence of new upholstery.

Upholstery can be complex or simple. Throw a rug on the grass at a picnic and you have performed a casual act of unofficial upholstery. For pre-historic cave-dwellers, a person-length mound of leaves, dried grass and sand, covered with an animal hide was probably their idea of padded luxury. Until the Industrial Revolution, standards of comfort in the form of upholstered furniture did not progress much for most of the population from these rudiments. For centuries, upholstery remained the preserve of the rich and powerful.

Opposite: Startling red velvet and gold calligraphy are used to great effect on a French-style armchair and two of London-based designer/ upholsterer, Carolyn Quartermaine's gilded dining chairs.

The uppercrust Egyptians, noble Romans and intellectual Greeks doubtless had mattresses and cushions to give comfort to their beds, thrones and stools, although little evidence remains today of covers or stuffing.

Medieval rulers were always on the move touring their estates and territories, so their possessions had to be portable. Upholstery pioneers in England were the cofferers who covered crudely made wooden chests and travelling trunks with leather and fabric. The task of hiding the coarse woodwork and joinery of ceremonial chairs beneath distinctive coverings naturally fell to these same craftsmen. In those times, chairs symbolised power and authority and few were made. A monarch had a throne, as did a bishop in his cathedral, and there were chairs of estate in feudal castles; lesser dignitaries sat, at best, on rough benches when at table in the great hall. Last of all came the masses who had little or no furniture.

As life became more settled, wealth spread beyond the court and the emerging domestic architecture became less fortress-like. Around the houses of the new landowners and merchants there were gardens instead of moats and drawbridges, while inside were many rooms to be filled with all types of furniture, not all of which were upholstered.

In the 17th century, British upholsterers (known until the 18th century as upholders) and woolen manufacturers, unsuccessfully petitioned parliament to suppress the manufacture and importation of light, cheap cane chairs. Originally from France and Holland, these simple cane chairs became much more elaborate when produced for the aristocracy. Although popular, canework was never really a substitute for lavish fabrics such as brocade, damask and figured velvet. Nor could it compete with the exquisite needlework on silk and wool, used on upholstered chairs. Trimmings were equally elaborate with braids incorporating silver and gold thread and brilliantly colored tassels and fringes. Thus a tradition developed whereby chair coverings greatly exceeded the value of their frames.

With the rise of the Puritans, the popularity of extravagant upholstery declined, only to re-emerge at double strength when the monarchy was reinstated.

Early in the Victorian era, Samuel Pratt's patented coiled spring put new bounce into chairs. This innovation was welcomed by the average consumer who rated comfort far above the mysteries of elegance, proportion and fine design. Romantic revivals of earlier furniture styles flourished, the most popular of which were Grecian, Gothic, Elizabethan and Louis XV, and elements from different eras were frequently intermingled. Interpretations of these and other influences, such as Flemish, Scottish, Saxon, Chinese, Egyptian and Jacobean, were often loosely rendered without historical accuracy.

Even when Victorian interiors were at their most turgid, new influences were at work. In the1860s and '70s, the Aesthetic movement championed art for art's sake, a return to craftsmanship and voiced strong disapproval of some of the excesses of Victorian decoration. At the same time,

Lyre-backed Sheraton-style sofa, upholstered in canary yellow trimmed with red and yellow cord with black-tasseled bolster – colors popular in the early 1800s which are equally appropriate today.

Japanese imports broadened the range of homewares in the west and paved the way for a renewed appreciation of grace and delicacy. Ten years before this, in Vienna, Thonet had developed upholstery-free furniture using steam to bend plywood and slender lengths of timber to great effect.

Because of improved economic and social conditions, by the end of the last century the market for furniture had expanded greatly. With more furniture for more people, upholstery boomed.

At the turn of the century, serious designer/craftsmen and the first industrial designers tried to make sense of the new methods and materials with varying degrees of success. Some of the fine designs of the Art Nouveau movement were commercially adapted in order to satisfy an undiscriminating market while others were produced according to design specifications but usually in limited numbers.

Left: Shapes, color and detailing from the past are re-worked in a modern context. Venetian red wool covers a winged and channeled armchair and buttoned ottoman.

Thus a pattern evolved, which still exists to a degree, of innovation and production of new designs, usually in small numbers, for specific clients at the top end of the market – the replacements for the kings, bishops and feudal rulers of old. Then there are several levels of mass production which cater to the rest of the market – from the bench-sitters, down.

At the mass market end there is the inevitable re-working of recognisable themes from the past (Queen Anne is a prime example) as well as the adaptation and re-interpretation of pieces created by the current design moguls. The time lapse is lessening between the release of a stunning furniture design and the idea being copied by others. In the past, years might elapse, but now, a design released at a furniture show can appear in the middle-market design and homemaking stores in a matter of months. By changing a design sufficiently to avoid copyright infringement, invariably some of the sense and impetus of the original is lost. The manufacturers are, however, interested in responding to the needs of their market for something new. Validity from a design point of view is generally a secondary concern.

In the midst of all this, there is the constant outpouring of ideas through interior decorating magazines. Fabric manufacturers, in particular, are constantly finding new and interesting ways of displaying their merchandise in advertisements that are sometimes more eye-catching than editorial features. In the best magazines, there is much to admire in the room sets and still lifes created by magazine stylists who, frequently with limited resources, alert us to new ways of combining furnishings and furniture. Also, by peeking into the houses of the rich, famous and talented through the pages of these same color magazines, much can be learned. The down side of this kind of design voyeurism is that it frequently raises hopes and expectations which cannot be fulfilled by those readers with little money to spend.

The purpose of this book is to celebrate the glories of fabric (and in one instance, leather) when used in upholstery, and to bridge the gap between the uninspired, run-of-the-mill furniture which most of us can afford, and the glamour in the palaces of corporate princes. From the following pictures and text you will discover how furniture which is outmoded or of little distinction, can be given dash and style with imaginative (and not necessarily expensive) upholstery.

INSPIRATION

New upholstery adds what I call 'star quality' to furniture by introducing new colors, patterns and trims. These pieces quickly become the main feature of their surrounding decor.

I used to think upholstery, new, old or in-between, was the single most elusive domestic luxury. Although adept at many home improvement tasks, upholstery had always eluded me. Eventually, I was driven to upholstery by a mixture of envy, frustration and curiosity because I felt it was high time I had better upholstery in my life.

Fine furniture from any era has never really had a place in my house. Most pieces have been either homemade, found, passed on to me or bought for a song.

The discovery, over 25 years ago, of a thick wad of money wrapped in a pair of tattered, denture-pink milanese scanties in the seat of an old chair first alerted me to the mysteries and riches of upholstery. This happened while living temporarily in a dwelling with a shopfront during the lull between fulltime child-rearing and re-launching a career. A friend had suggested starting a furniture and bric-à-brac business so we applied for a secondhand dealer's licence. My partner-to-be, a fledgling journalist from London, soon began writing freelance for newspapers and magazines. Then I too eased my

Above: What next? Chairs awaiting upholstery.
Opposite: Familiar meets modern with a golden may tree leaf print on a chunky armchair.

way back into similar work so the furniture business was abandoned by mutual consent. The dealer's licence lapsed soon after.

The chair in question was hers, bought for a few dollars at a local junk store. I confirmed that the old ten shilling and pound notes were, in fact, real and still legal tender.

Since then, I have only found hair pins, confectionery wrappers, dust, vermin and pet hair in furniture I have stripped. Needless to say, I live in hope of finding another stash of money.

It is not difficult to acquire a taste for glamorous upholstery. The combination of colors, patterns and textures in the fabrics alone is sufficient. Then the generous contours beneath the fabric will work their magic spell on homemakers who yearn for beauty and comfort.

This general appreciation of upholstery, and particularly furniture upholstered with fabric, has gradually gathered momentum since the beginning of this decade. Prior to this, leather was the preferred cover for modern furniture. Manufacturers who used to produce up to 90% of their stock in

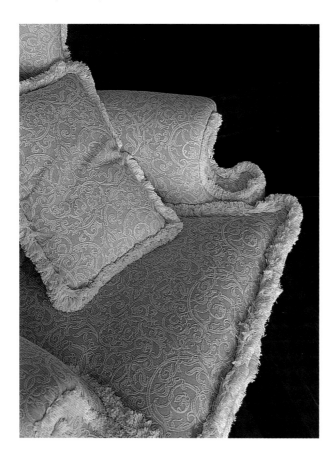

Above: Fringing replaces
the usual crisp line of
piping with a friendly
fluffy edge.
Opposite: The weight of
high-backed dining chairs
is greatly reduced by
modern materials such
as foam.

leather now report that fabric far outstrips hide in popularity.

Today, like most other periods of furniture design, the acknowledgement and reverence for tradition, as well as a healthy appreciation of the new, give the furniture patron much from which to choose. Comfort is certainly a high priority so it is unlikely there will be a revival of the severe designs of the Modern Movement which started in 1914. Then only straight lines were employed and structural elements were never disguised by fabric, springs or padding. By contrast, the most intense era for upholstery was at the close of Victoria's reign when some chairs were so deeply buttoned and fringed that the notion of structure was almost denied. Our present path lies somewhere between these two extremes.

Currently, the least appealing furniture seems to be that of the recent past, such as the mournful, black imitation leather easy chairs of the seventies which don't rate the cost of transportation to the next home and are tipped onto the street on moving day. No one ever wants them. Also in profusion are the teak dining chairs of the sixties and seventies with oatmeal-colored vinyl or neutral-toned 'Berber' wool upholstery. As you'll see on the following pages, even the most depressing pieces can be redeemed with new upholstery. In cases such as these where there is no point pursuing fine design, the best plan is to have some fun and resort to the art of disguise.

If, however, you are in the market for something new in upholstered furniture, there are several points worth bearing in mind. Because foam has replaced much of the heavier padding and springs associated with traditional upholstery, quite solid-looking pieces, such as high-backed fully upholstered dining chairs, are often surprisingly light. For most of us, it is the outer appearance that is the prime concern although some thought should be given to the inner workings because it is here, mostly, that price is determined.

Foam is a miracle material because it is cheap, easy to shape, and can be glued or stapled into position. At an upholstery supply shop you will see it in many different grades, from soft through to firm. Used alone, it can take the place of springs and padding and the invention of fire retardant foam has checked its flammability. In the USA, foam and all other upholstery materials have to conform to the strict fire retardancy regulations. In countries and states without these laws, it is still highly advisable to use fire retardant materials.

In the interests of practicality, this modern factory-produced sofa has washable cotton zip-off covers for bolsters and seat, back and scatter cushions. The soft profile of the seat comes from a down-filled undercover.

A typical modern medium to expensively priced sofa, such as the one above, is not of the lightweight variety even though foam is a major component. It has a solid timber structure shrouded in foam for the back and sides and two tubular steel stretchers (braces) between the front rail and the lower back for strength. Instead of springs, the foam seat slab is supported by very tough, slightly elasticised synthetic webbing. The seat cushion is medium density foam with denser foam strips, triangular in section, glued to the front and back edges of the cushion top. (The triangular strip of foam toughens the cushion's edge.) Over this, a zippered, down-filled cover gives comfort and a soft profile to the seat cushion. Foam forms the scroll arm which compresses alarmingly if sat on. Where the arm meets the seat, the width of the timber framing can be gauged; above this line, foam accounts for all the shaping.

The Indian cotton cover was placed straight over the foam and stapled to the underside of the frame and the legs screwed into the base. Bolster cushions are polyester fibrefill; other cushions are down filled. All cushion and armrest covers can be removed for laundering, which makes sense with a light-colored fabric. The only fixed upholstery is on the back, sides and lower front platform.

Sofas of this type are built in a factory with each stage of production assigned to specific teams. Most upholstery training these days is aimed at those who will be employed in furniture factories.

The solid back and sides of this mass-produced model hark back to medieval times when chairs were primitive developments of the chests used for storage and transport of valuables. The modern rationale for this is the ease with which foam can be stapled to solid timber.

A traditional upholsterer is a highly skilled tradesman or woman who can build sofas in a number of styles. Commission a modern one and he or she would order a much more skeletal frame from a specialist maker who would shape it to express the scroll shape of the arm, sides and back. It would be built from strong, well-seasoned lengths of timber which are knot free. For strength and stability, the legs would be lower extensions of the frame sides and not screwed on at the end. The inner back, sides and seat would be webbed, sprung, covered with hessian and stuffed with material such as moss or curled animal hair. Over this a layer of cotton wadding would be laid, which may even be followed by a softening outer padding of down, enclosed and channeled in japarra – a tightly woven featherproof fabric with a slightly waxy, crackly finish. Outer back and sides would be less elaborately padded with cotton wadding supported by hessian tacked to the frame. Over all of this, an undercover of unbleached cotton would be tacked to take the strain off the upholstery fabric. Any cushions would be down filled, perhaps with a core of foam for its shape-retaining qualities. Naturally, the cost of the time, materials and labor (40 to 60 hours) involved would make the custom-made sofa at least five times more expensive than the price of the factory-built version.

Demand for traditional upholstery is alive and well in Europe and the USA where there is a reverence for the skills of the past. There are also plenty of fine antiques in need of repair and conservation. In societies less well endowed with fine furniture and good intentions, those with the ability to upholster in the traditional way are quickly disappearing. Apprentices cannot be attracted to the trade and local sources of materials, such as curled horse and cattle hair, are closing down. Hopefully, a resurgence in traditional trades and crafts will grip the globe and all those in possession of the skills of the past will once again be in demand and amply rewarded for their labors.

Where you shop for upholstered furniture depends entirely on your budget. Before deciding on a custom upholsterer, furniture retailer, antique shop, clearance house or junk market, it may be useful to ponder the options. These cover a broad range of tastes and it is worth acquainting yourself fully with the many types of treatments available.

DIFFERENT APPROACHES

It is interesting to see how design professionals furnish and decorate their homes. Fashion houses and big-name designers have reputations for invading the home scene. We have become quite used to 'home' being added to the labels we associate with the catwalk and presume this is an attempt to seek longevity for their products.

Although homewares and furnishings do have fashion aspects and are often marketed and promoted as such, typical consumers are happy to see fabric and furniture designs endure for many seasons. Those that do stand the test of time become classics which continue to be produced, much to the delight of their originators. But rarely is there traffic the other way, with the luminaries of interior design pushing their luck in the rag trade.

Fabric is the common denominator of fashion and furnishing and so it is not surprising that a childrenswear designer/manufacturer, Rae Ganim, has brought her wealth of personal talent and experience to the furnishing world. It all began in her own house when she took to her rather chunky cream sofas with brush and fabric paint, turning them into illustrated furniture. In parts they are densely worked. Sometimes the painting trails off leaving just bare 'canvas' and a few sensuously drawn lines. On the long stool, the image starts at one end with swirling plants (or are they sea creatures?) that soon give way to the bold stripes of a circus tent, but in several colors.

She also took a green and red floral fabric, one of her past designs for a summer clothing range, and made slip-over covers for a

Below: Handpainted striped ottoman with squiggly motifs.

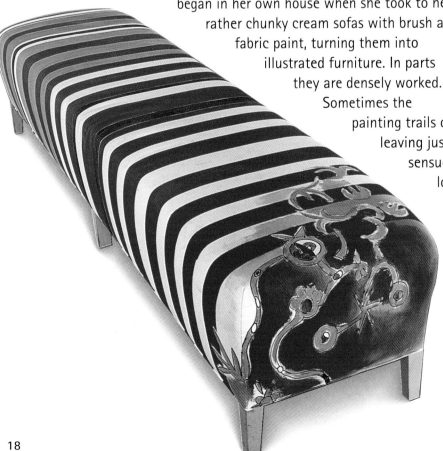

set of directors chairs. Apart from the brilliant choice of fabric, it is the middy length of the covers, which permits a coy glimpse of leg and cross brace, that lends these chairs such distinction and style. So often, covers for these simple chairs can merely repeat a cliché.

Encouraged by an interior design shop, she has painted fabric for sofas and sets of seat and floor cushions. Choosing a white backgound, she selected what she calls a very serious sofa shape, as opposed to her own more dumpy models, so the painting has maximum impact.

Left: Illustrated sofa by Rae Ganim.
Below: On the rear of the sofa, painting trails off in parts leaving patches of bare 'canvas'.
Overleaf: Adjacent painted sofas.

A cache of old necktie fabrics (some pure silk and some rayon) was the inspiration for the upholstery pictured here. A couturier with a nose for the unusual found a shipment which had been overlooked at a warehouse and bought a selection with her own furniture in mind. Ties will only hang properly if they are cut on the bias. Therefore, the fabric from which ties are cut is always designed so the pattern 'reads' properly in this diagonal direction; an interesting challenge for an upholsterer.

On the sofa shown here, the fabrics are exquisitely 'layered', the tempo of their different designs working together from the floor up like intricate bands of Middle Eastern tiles. Mortals with less courage than this fearless fashioner of society frocks would have baulked at this exercise, but the result is one of complex and agreeable harmony – apparently an effortless combination of color and complicated pattern. The rectangular shapes and flattish planes of the furniture are the perfect foil for such a cacophony of design elements.

The fabrics work equally well on the witchy-pooh dining chairs with their carved cat heads. Although there is less opportunity for multiple combinations, three different patterns for the seat, inside back and outside back make a handsome statement. This system of compound pattern also works its special spell on the piano stool seen on the next page. The beautifully carved and painted upright piano is obviously the hero of this duo. However, the stool puts up a good show of strength with several different patterns of fabric embracing the gold, green, tan, cream and white theme. Note how the diamond checks on the legs hint at the diverse angles of the elaborately carved piano legs.

Main picture: Well-dressed sofa covered with several different necktie fabrics.
Left and above: Cat chair outfitted in necktie fabrics.
Overleaf: Piano stool in a variety of fabrics with diamond checked legs.

THRIFT STORE FURNITURE

Lack of funds never seems to limit those amongst the young who have the wit and talent to seek beauty in simpler, modestly priced things. Fortunately, style is not always dependent on wealth. A daybed with a wooden swing back and curved arms, a standard piece of furniture on the verandahs of suburban houses in the fifties, has been elevated here to inner-city living room status. First, the timber was stripped and refinished with clear polyurethane. For the seat cushion, a white linen cover was made with a pleated front panel reaching the floor. This hid the mesh spring base of the daybed and also served to impart a restrained air of formality. Square cushions have green hessian fronts and linen backs. Bolsters in an ikat fabric have gathered ends with piped edges.

In the same house, a bulky armchair is draped with a reverse colorway of the daybed bolster fabric (actually a tablecloth this time), in calm anticipation of a transformation at a future date. Good intentions may eventually lapse into 'unfinished symphonies' but are an important step in any decorating plan. It is much better to 'test drive' the effect of the fabric like this and determine its worth than to make a snap decision that could be entirely wrong, and costly as well.

Above: Armchair draped with ikat tablecloth awaits upholstery.
Right: Verandah daybed from the fifties era is modestly covered and cushioned for its current life indoors.

DINING CHAIRS

Six, eight, ten or more chairs, all the same – the dining room is unique in that it is home to a mass of look-alike pieces of furniture. If the chairs themselves are a little dull, it seems a pity to underscore this by dressing them in safe, look-alike upholstery.

The convention of having matched seating in the dining room was challenged years ago by nonconformists who surrounded their tables with a mixture of chairs. In those rule-testing rooms, the mood in general was informal, the table pine, and the chairs of the grass-seated, kitchen or bentwood variety. People who preferred upholstered chairs usually opted for uniformity of furniture style and upholstery fabric.

Modern dining chairs with fully upholstered backs and seats are now enjoying great popularity. Although the woodwork is invariably without embellishment, the basic shape has much in common with early Georgian side chairs; variations of these graceful classics have been produced for centuries. The modern-day versions found favor in the eighties, in

Top: Three different colors for three identical chairs. Above: Modern dining chair in a skin-tight zippered two-piece cover.

restaurants and establishments keen to promote an atmosphere of ease and elegance, before they moved into the domestic scene.

Today, with a broader cross-section of people interested in upholstered dining chairs, more adventurous treatments in fabric and trim are to be seen. A fabric with a particularly strong design may be used to bring harmony to a group of mis-matched chairs. Or on the other hand, a clutch of colorways of the one fabric could inject variety and interest into a dining room full of identical chairs. Techniques of trimming with fringes, tassels, bows and brass nails, and of tufting with leather discs, wound thread or buttons, may be varied on a set of chairs in an attempt to ascertain the perfect finish. Along the way they may be left as they are if the variation-on-a-theme turns out to be the desired effect.

Silks, cottons, wools, linens, synthetics and combinations of these are the fabrics most often associated with dining chair upholstery. Woven grass and cane make marvelous upholsteries for rather formal dining chairs, perhaps because they openly trade on the element of surprise (beach hut meets city apartment). The unexpected is happily accompanied by other qualities, such as their seductive textures and warm natural colors which should not be overlooked.

Usually the preserve of classy decorators, woven grass and palm leaf 'fabric' is sometimes available as beach mats which are quite inexpensive. It may well be worth experimenting with matting on a very simply shaped chair, remembering that a misting of water will make the material much easier to bend.

Below: Formal shape of a scroll dining chair responds elegantly to the natural texture of woven cane.

THE RELAXED LOOK

Perhaps one of the most agreeable things to happen to upholstery in recent years is the arrival of the relaxed look which gives chairs and sofas a cosy, lived-in, slightly shabby air. This followed in the footsteps of an appreciation for 'distressed' furniture and interiors champion-ing aged elegance. But there are boundaries beyond which shabby chic passes quickly into decrepitude – a thin film of dust is acceptable, a layer of fat-trapped grime is not.

Fabric manufacturers, who have toiled in the past to produce wrinkle-free fabrics, now have ranges which wrinkle deliberately. This is all of particular interest to the home-sewing maker of

The over-sized, piping-free cover on this modern armchair has the unstructured appeal of a loose-fitting dress.

These plain and plaid loose covers are as friendly and inviting as a favorite pair of slippers.

slipcovers who has probably been pioneering this look unintentionally for years. But there is always a catch. Although relaxed loose covers no longer have to fit like sausage skins, the aim is for an eased look all over and not pulled in one part and floppy in another. The least complicated way of achieving this effect is with an over-sized, piping-free cover on a simple, modern chair or sofa. It will hang like a sack dress.

When it is time to wash a loose-fitting cover, put it back on the chair when it is still a little damp. You don't need to iron it.

COLORS and PATTERNS

Show staid upholstery the door and welcome a new, bold face on padded furniture. Checks have never been so outrageous, but they are adaptable enough to heighten the effect of sensuous curves, as well as conform to the lines of more boxy pieces.

If using strong patterns such as these, it is as well to think about where it is all going to stop. By keeping the fabric off the ground and keeping your chair or sofa skirt-free, you will give 'breathing space' to the piece. The eye will travel along the floor uninterrupted and the piece of furniture will not appear to consume more than its fair share of the room. This is also a good plan to follow in small areas where creating a sense of space is the main objective.

One boldly patterned piece does not have to be the only source of interest in a room. It could be a thrilling departure point for more pattern still. Many fabric firms have taken much of the hard work out of 'mixing' by producing extensive ranges with go-together colors and designs. But you can be a free agent, do your own co-ordinating and pick and choose from them all. Take a broadly brush-stroked check fabric and make it the main ingredient for a pattern 'pie' with stripes and dots.

If it works well, it feels good and engages you like a catchy tune. With decisions such as these, you are the judge and jury; trust yourself.

Left: Wing and arm front curves carve out chunks of the bold plaid fabric, which serve to heighten the sensuous lines of this chair.

Right: The brushstroked checks, dots and stripes on cushion, bolster and daybed are all linked by the color blue.

Overleaf: In a spacious loft against a backdrop of black-banded window panes, exposed bricks and pale timber floor, fabrics impose bold color in checks, stripes, plains and diamonds.

In pursuit of this kind of layering of pattern, there is a good case for combining two or more fabrics on one chair. With a color link of the perpetually popular blue and white, success is assured. The choice of a scattered foliage pattern with stripes provides pleasant variation without confrontation.

Pattern can work its magic within the framework of apparently plain color. Take deep-buttoning for instance. Championed by the Victorians to anchor the generous stuffing in their chairs and sofas, it pulls fabric into regular depressions, usually taking the form of diamonds defined by pleats. The fabric cover is carefully calculated to allow for the extra taken up by dips

Above: The art of pattern mixing delicately executed in blue and white stripes and leaves. Right: Deep buttoning performed in brilliant colors on plain white.

Over-the-top floral upholstery with huge blooms covers everything on this sofa.

and rises, and much plotting and planning of the buttons goes on before they are sewn through the fabric and tied off. Then the fabric has to find its way to the outer edge of the buttoned piece and this is usually done from the outside row of buttons via deep channels in the stuffing into which the fabric is pleated. With a white cover and buttons in an array of bright paintbox hues, a spirited rhythm of pattern and color is artfully established.

One of the most popular subjects for the conveyance of color and pattern in upholstery is the flower. Florals have been equally patronised and maligned by arbiters of taste, but the detractors have failed to dampen the general enthusiasm for furniture with floral upholstery. Whether the motifs are stylised and tiny so that they tap out a regular dot design, or blowzy to an almost indecent degree, floral fabric continues to bloom unchecked in vast numbers of conservative as well as radical interiors. Imaginative renditions in upholstery can exploit the excesses of floral imagery with bigger-than-ever-before blooms that envelop a whole chair – legs included.

SLIPCOVERS

Right: This tassel-topped
slim-fitting cover extends
an invitation to be seated
– many times over. Chairs
motifs, ancient and
modern, rustic and slick,
are printed on cotton..
Below: A sober armchair's
romantic summer garb is
piped and frilled with a
plain blue border.
Opposite: Slipcovers
in gently shaded stripes
evoke the essence of
romance.

Used today principally to disguise worn or outdated upholstery, slipcovers were once regarded as being far inferior to upholstery but very necessary as a protection for it. In the affluent dining rooms of the distant past, neatly tailored slip-on covers for chairs were made by the household staff. Decorated with embroidered crests, insignias or family initials, these coverings were only removed for special occasions when the sumptuous upholstery fabric was revealed in all its glory. Later, in Victorian times, it was customary, in warmer weather, to conceal the dark upholsteries of chairs and sofas with printed floral covers. Heavy Victorian window treatments would also be lightened and brightened with summery curtains.

Nowadays, instead of being the housecoat to upholstery's ball gown grandeur, slipcovers are often a rescue measure for dated or worn chairs and sofas. Or, when new furniture is sold with a cream cotton undercover

such as calico (muslin in the US), a slipcover may be the preferred method of 'dressing' the piece. The covers themselves can be trim fitting or relaxed, subtle or strong, exotic or humble, depending on the required effect.

If antiquity appeals, imitate dining chair covers of a bygone era and embellish plain linen or cotton with embroidered, stencilled or painted initials, signs, symbols or numbers.

Documentary fabrics are constantly being revived from the archives and printed anew for those who like to soften the harsh realities of modern life with patterns of the past.

A slipcover can dramatically alter a chair's appearance. Covers with long skirts instantly transform ordinary dining chairs into objects of romance. So popular is this method of lending formality and softness to utility, that it has been embraced by party hire firms who dress metal stacking chairs in frills and frippery.

Right: Beige square-line
sofa has been tied over
with a three-piece
lavender tabard.
Below: Back interest is
desirable when a chair is
turned away from the
main action of a room.

Usually it is bland, modern furniture which can most be helped by loose covers. Consider the plight of a square-line, beige covered two-seater. Dress it with a three-piece lavender tabard (lined with beige) that gives a frontal glimpse of the existing fabric. Anchor the panels of the cover with emerald green ties and trim lavender cushions with green piping and buttons. The transformation is remarkable.

Light-colored fabrics, however appealing, risk becoming quickly soiled and are therefore impractical for most fully fitted upholstery projects. This is especially true in households with small children and pets. For a loose cover, a washable pale fabric is absolutely ideal. Have it baggy and un-structured with a minimum of trim, semi-slack but enhanced with crewel embroidery, or tightly fitted with zips and Velcro®.

If a slip-covered chair is ever likely to turn its back on the main action in the room to address a view or face a fire, some thought should be given to its backview. Buttons attached in pairs like cuff links could draw the centre backs together over an inverted pleat. Or toggles could be used in the same way. Ties made from the cover fabric, or silk or cotton cord, would also be an improvement on machine-stitched zippers.

On dining chairs, by using ties or hook and loop tape (Velcro®) and cutting and seaming carefully, loose covers need not be loose at all; they can look just like upholstery. Where much is made of setting the scene for cele-brations, the dining room could be dressed up by co-ordinating new chair covers with decorations and the table setting for festive occasions.

Right: A startling print
will set a chair apart for
special attention.

If you are inclined to romance or want to a pursue a comfortable,
country theme, then slipcovers are far more appropriate than fitted
upholstery. To capture the mood, start with classic-shaped chairs and sofas
and have skirted, loose-fitting covers in full-blown florals, tiny flower-
sprigged prints, checks, ticking stripes and/or plain fabrics. A judicious mix
of patterns and plains with a color link (however slight) that is common to
all is a well-tried recipe for success in this kind of environment.

One of the nicest ways of using a slipcover is to set a chair apart for
special attention, to define it as the specific property of the most senior or
deserving member of the family. The chair itself must be comfortable to the
point of decadence and preferably with a matching footstool. Have it
facing the view, the fire or beside the best reading light, and sited off the
main traffic path in a draft-free zone. Make the cover in the chairholder's
favorite color, pattern and fabric, with perhaps a large patch pocket on the
outside arm for reading material, knitting and spectacles. Plump it with
cushions that fill any nooks and crannies to perfection.

PROFESSIONAL UPHOLSTERERS

When I started to upholster furniture, I used to root around for stuffing and hardware at specialist stores and upholstery wholesalers, never daring, as a mere pretender to the trade, to approach a local upholsterer.

After countless inquiries, I still couldn't locate curled horse hair and, wherever I asked, I was told that it wasn't used any more.

Horse hair for upholstery stuffing comes from the manes and tails of horses, is carefully graded by length then twisted into skeins and dunked in a kind of perming lotion. When dried, unravelled and teased out by hand, it provides the characteristic body and bounce expected by traditionalists in their upholstered furniture. It can be used on sprung and un-sprung chairs and is usually topped with a layer of softer cotton padding before the fixing of the unbleached cotton undercover and, finally, the upholstery fabric.

The supply of old horse hair mattresses at jumble sales and markets, which used to keep professionals and amateurs in stock, has almost disappeared. Re-using hair from old furniture and bedding is a common practice; it is washed, dried and teased again so it regains its original resilience.

I eventually traced the co-owner of the last hair curling plant on this continent which had ceased production and was just about to close. He was well past retiring age and had been trying without success to sell his firm for the last seven years. I learnt from this veteran of the

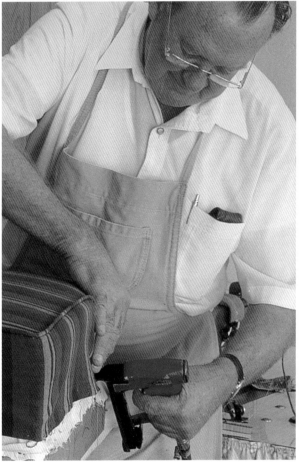

Retirement held little appeal for this veteran of the furniture business so he started up his own one-man upholstery shop in the suburbs and is back at work full time.

curled hair trade that, in recent years, horse hair had become difficult to obtain locally so his product consisted mainly of hair from cattle tails. The best horse tails are now made into 'falsies' for show ponies. These tail extensions are woven into a host horse's own tail and no one knows the difference in the show ring.

Driven by curiosity, I overcame my reticence and tracked down a top quality upholsterer who regularly does work for historic houses through a firm of furniture and fine arts conservators. He treasured his store of curled hair and would not part with any of it, for any price.

COVERING THE SEAT OF A DROP-IN DINING CHAIR

1 With padding and springs in good condition, base of seat was reinforced with four new strips of webbing.

2 Velvet cover set in place, stretched taut and stapled first on opposite centres of all four sides.

3 After working from centres out, fabric is pulled, snipped, folded and stapled to form neat corners.

4 The finished seat has the nap of the velvet running from the back of the seat to the front.

He had sufficient to last him until he retires in the near future to run a small hotel in France. He was not yet 50. He suggested that I approach a specialist supplier from whom he had bought his last lot of curled hair. Alas, the person I spoke to when I phoned this place said that they had never stocked curled hair. The ranks were closing.

Another tack-and-hammer upholsterer of the same age in another capital city had no such exotic retirement plans but was equally protective of his supply of curled hair. He had enough to last him for a while, but where would the next lot come from?

At other less specialised upholstery workshops, inquiries about curled hair met with shaking heads. The senior tradespeople had not seen it around for at least 20 years. They did their traditional upholstery with coir fibre over

PADDING A STOOL

1 Hessian conceals jute webbing and is being stitched with bridle ties using twine and a curved packing needle.

2 First handful of teased-out cotton flocking is slipped under bridle tie, parted and taken right to the corner's edge.

3 Each subsequent handful is kneaded with those already in place so the padding becomes even and well blended.

4 The outer limits of the stool are heaped with cotton flocking which is restrained by the bridle ties.

5 Coir fibre pads the centre of the stool. It is picked over and fluffed up by hand before being positioned.

6 With the sides and centre paddings in place, a further layer of flocking goes over the top.

7 Unconfined padding seems very high but will be reduced by a third when constrained by the cover.

the springs, followed by cotton flocking, then linters or polyester wadding. Cotton flocking is a fluffy substance which is a clean waste product from the garment trade and linters is a raw cotton by-product from the cotton gin, which is felted into loosely packed sheets and rolled around a paper strip into bales. When requested by a client for whom tradition is important, they use tacks only on the undersides of chairs. Under normal circumstances, the fixing is done with staples. Tacks are used as temporary fixings (they are only partially hammered in) when stretching a section of fabric on a chair to check the fit but are removed after stapling.

In a furniture factory priding itself on modern manufacturing, I was told about the tendency amongst some furniture makers to romanticise their methods of construction in advertisements by

Selection from a professional upholsterer's tool kit. The bat-shaped tool on the left is a webbing stretcher and against it leans a trimming knife. Next, is a ripping chisel for removing tacks and staples with a tack hammer beside it. The bull-nosed pliers to the lower right of the hammer are used to strain and tighten short lengths of webbing. Massive upholstery shears are beautifully balanced. Rasp at the bottom is for smoothing out sharp edges and splinters in timber. Upholstery skewers are on the bottom flap of the green felt needle case with two double-ended bayonet needles to the right, then a regulator and finally a curve-ended packing needle at the far right. At the top there is a wooden mallet which is used with a ripping chisel to strip off old upholstery and remove tacks, and beneath are pincers for removing stubborn or broken tacks and staples from furniture.

showing white-haired craftsmen with half-moon glasses using hammers to drive in tacks. In reality, their workshops are more likely to be staffed by youngish people fixing foam to frames with air-powered staple or tack guns. Staples can do more than fasten upholstery; in modern chair construction, 10 cm (4 in) staples with adhesive are frequently used in place of traditional dowelled joints. Power nailing with serrated shank nails, which are similar to screws, is another joining technique used in modern furniture construction.

WHAT CAN YOU LEARN FROM THE PROFESSIONALS?

More than anything else, it is the speed with which tasks are accomplished in an upholstery workshop which impresses the amateur. Upholsterers never have to look at a diagram of a slip knot before tying one and stitch bridle ties into hessian under which stuffing is positioned in a flash.

In order to unpick a long seam efficiently, a senior upholsterer devised a simple method of holding a length of fabric taut. He drilled a small hole in the edge of one end of his work bench and uses an upholstery skewer to fasten the fabric to the table. While pulling the free end of the fabric tight, he can swiftly rip away the seam stitching with a stitch unpicker.

This same tradesman keeps the cotton flocking he is using for a specific project in a basket and stirs it with a stick occasionally. This fluffs up the material, stops it from lumping and makes it easier to tease out by hand prior to building up a padded surface on a chair. Although there is much to learn by observing the professionals at work, their expertise should not intimidate the novice; one can take heart at the occasional prising out of tacks or staples when a mistake is made.

Air powered tools take much of the hand strain out of upholstering but because they run on compressed air, these tools require a considerable investment. As well as easy-to-use staple guns, there are amazing cylindrical hole boring attachments for drills which make perfect holes in foam for deep buttoning. Adhesive spray guns are also air powered and are used for bonding foam slabs together. The glue is tinted red so the upholsterer can see where the spray has landed. (For the home upholsterer, foam adhesive can be bought in spray cans although it is not tinted.)

Work benches are at different levels for different jobs – at work-bench height for upholstering bed heads and dismantled seats and backs and 45 cm (18 in) above the ground for chairs and sofas. There is always a piece of foam, felt or fabric on the bench to protect the furniture when it is being upholstered.

The cleaning up routine is very much a matter of personal preference and opinions vary as to how often the workshop should be cleaned and tidied. Some subscribe to the view that once a week, usually on Friday afternoon, is sufficient and the rest of the time it is fairly chaotic. Others pride themselves on having an orderly working environment at all times.

The machinist always works with very accurately cut fabric. For an amateur it is marvelous to see the top of a cushion being sewn to a boxing strip (side panel) without pins. The machinist simply snips at the edge of the strip just prior to turning a corner and it all fits together as if by magic, and at high speed.

A walking foot on an industrial sewing machine is a wonderful thing to behold. If you sew two long lengths of fabric together on an ordinary sewing machine, the top piece invariably ends up longer than the bottom piece. This is because the feed teeth grab the underside of the fabric while the stitching foot stretches the top fabric creating inequality between the two, over distance. A walking foot lifts up after every stitch and sets down on the fabric again when the needle pierces the fabric. This motion evens out the traction on the top and bottom fabrics resulting in evenness of length after sewing.

COVERING AN ARMCHAIR

1 Trimming a layer of polyester wadding on the outer arm.

2 Stapling the outside arm cover in place.

3 Measuring fabrics and padding for outside back.

4 Stapling hessian in place; note turned-under seam allowance.

5 Chair on floor with wadding covering hessian and metal tacking strip cut to size.

6 Tacking strip is stapled to seam line of outside back.

7 Cover fabric is slip tacked to the lower back chair rail and then poked into the jaws of the tacking strip with a regulator.

8 Excess fabric is trimmed away from edges of the outside back.

9 Small cardboard strip softens blows from tack hammer as strip is flattened and fabric stretched taut.

GETTING STARTED

It is improbable that anyone attempting upholstery at home will make an in-depth study of professional upholstery techniques. What is more likely to happen is that you will appraise the task ahead, find the required materials and tools and, to the best of your ability, do it.

The sequence of work, the specialised knots, the various ways of anchoring stuffing – all the methods devised by professionals who have to make upholstery pay are indispensable in the upholstery workshop. It is worthwhile for the amateur to acquire some knowledge of accepted upholstery techniques, but you can get by, to a degree, with just a few basics.

I have never done an upholstery course, but I am interested in how things work, and I can sew. The books in my collection of upholstery texts come from both the UK and the USA, and sometimes terminology and techniques vary. For instance, a 'stretcher' in an American book is a strip of inexpensive fabric sewn to the cover which is used as an extension for the fastening process of tacking or stapling. This stretcher is hidden from view and is an economy measure, saving on the cost of upholstery fabric. A stretcher in the UK is a supporting rod of straight or curved steel, or a timber rail placed at 60 cm (24 in) centres between the front and back seat rails of a sofa. In the US, the British stretcher is called a brace. And the British calico is the American muslin. Muslin in the UK is a plain weave sheer cotton. Calico in the US is printed, whereas calico in the UK is plain and usually unbleached. Despite differences of terminology and variations in methods, it is usually not difficult to work out what is meant on both sides of the Atlantic.

The main differences in upholstery are not, however, to do with location and perplexing terminology, but in choice of technique – traditional versus modern, curled hair versus foam, tack-and-hammer versus the staple gun. The method selected will depend on the available funds, availability of materials, personal taste and, if you are doing it yourself, your own level of skill. Traditional techniques and materials are usually reserved for antiques whilst foam is used on modern pieces. However, there are exceptions to both these propositions with modern pieces being upholstered in the old way, and antiques in the new.

Upholstery is a natural link between sewing and woodwork because it requires elements of both and will gradually introduce anyone who is mildly competent in either craft to a complementary skill. If you are interested in learning about upholstery, enroll in a course by all means. But if you, like me, feel that a few hours over a number of weeks will not be a satisfactory period in which to complete a task, investigate the alternatives, such as weekend workshops. (I would much rather devote every waking hour to a project until it is finished than drag it out.)

Another option to a course is to approach the proprietor of a local upholstery shop; he or she may be willing to take you on in a voluntary capacity as a work experience candidate.

THE HOME WORK SPACE

There will no doubt be a degree of compromise as far as creating the ideal work space at home is concerned. Upholstery usually has to be a secondary function of a room and not its sole purpose.

Wherever you locate your home upholstery work space, good light, both natural and artificial, is imperative. The floor and work surfaces should be easily cleaned and sturdy enough to endure the scuffing, dings and bangs that inevitably occur in the course of an upholstery project.

Some tasks, such as the stripping of old, dust-impregnated upholstery may best be done outside, preferably on a table so the work is elevated and the worker does not have to stoop continually.

For pieces such as single chairs and bed heads, I tend to work on the kitchen table; the corner of the table gives 270° access to the upturned seat of a dining chair. With office chairs, the pedestal or stand usually screws off so you don't have to cope with the full height of the chair on the work table.

With a sofa, you will probably have to work on the floor. I find the carpeted floor of my sitting room is more comfortable than a hard floor because much of the time is spent kneeling. For those who have tender knees, work pants with padded knees (upholstered trousers!) are a good idea. In my experience, rubber strap-on knee pads stay in place for only a matter of minutes before sliding down to the calves. You can never just pull them up; they have to be unbuckled, re-aligned and tightened up all over again.

A professional upholstery workshop always has a machinist who does the sewing. Although some upholsterers can sew, usually the machinists cannot or will not do upholstery. At home, there is no such division of labor; you will most likely do everything.

My sewing centre is in the sitting room (one floor above the kitchen) with my 30 year old portable sewing machine on a 75 x 220 cm (about 30 in x 7½ ft) desk, bought at a warehouse clearance sale. A good anglepoise lamp with a halogen globe lights the work at night as I find the overhead illumination and the light in the machine are too weak. I position the head of the lamp above and to the left of the stitching plate for maximum brightness.

When not in use, the machine is concealed beneath a cover made from a cast-off green velvet altar cloth, which keeps off the dust and makes a mild aesthetic contribution to the room.

Sometimes the desk becomes a cutting surface but I am more likely to use the floor when lots of fabric is involved. It is much easier to cut out on a non-slippery surface.

A furnishing professional will most likely have a huge padded work table, large enough to spread out a couple of widths of fabric, set centrally in the room so it can be approached from all sides. The surface is good to work on and will easily accept pins and a hot iron. The sewing machine is usually located nearby but not on the work table. Such luxury of space is unlikely to occur in the average home but some enthusiasts devise fold-away temporary tops for kitchen or dining tables which provide some of the features of the professional work table.

My own upholstery tool set. Tack hammer has improvised leather 'nose cone' to protect decorative upholstery nails. Webbing stretcher (lower right) comes with a cardboard guard for the prongs. Directly above the claw hammer there are brown gimp pins on the right and tacks on the left. Laidcord, a tough man-made twine, is on the top left, beside the coil of jute webbing. Hot glue gun is top right with red staple gun below.

TOOLS

My motley selection of tools comes from the family tool kit which contains equipment used for the usual household repairs and renovations. It was only in the closing moments of this book that I bought a webbing stretcher, a tacking hammer and a hot glue gun. Prior to this, I had only ever replaced the odd strip of webbing and accomplished this with the help of an extra pair of hands. A family member would take the loose end of the webbing between the jaws of a pair of needle-nosed (radio) pliers, and pull it tight while I stapled it to the chair rail.

The first time I used my new tack hammer, I hit my finger, broke the skin and bled on the leather upholstery of a dining chair. The blood was quickly removed with a damp cloth.

Learning to use the hot glue gun was not without incident either. It seemed to take ages to get used to the rate of flow of the glue. I was always applying too little or too much. The glue sets very quickly so work has to be well prepared and trims put hastily into place once the glue is applied. Where it dried too quickly, I tried re-aligning the trim and bonding it with a hot iron which again melts the glue. This can be satisfactory, but if the line of glue is too thick and the trim is narrow, it can melt out beyond the trim and become visible.

At the beginning, the instruction leaflet advised using two sticks of glue for the first operation. I took this hint literally, tried to force in the first one to make way for the second and accidentally started a Niagara of hot glue from the nozzle which burnt my hand.

Once mastered, the hot glue gun is a useful tool but the learning process can be painful. Do several test runs to perfect the technique before using the gun for fixing trims on furniture and always keep it well away from children and novices.

I have not yet bought a ripping chisel or mallet; the tools recommended for stripping upholstery and removing tacks and staples from furniture. Instead I use a medium-sized screwdriver and find that when a staple is particularly stubborn, it sometimes helps to tackle it from the other side. Staples are often put in at an angle and 'bite' more on one side than the other. To remove leftover bits of staples and tacks which protrude from wood, use pincers, snips or small pliers.

Early in my upholstery career, I was devoted to my needle-nosed pliers and used them constantly. They were lost for quite some time and eventually I became accustomed to doing without them; for a while a pair of ordinary medium-sized pliers took their place.

My attachment to those needle-nosed pliers may have been superficial, but no such error of judgment exists regarding my feelings for my staple gun.

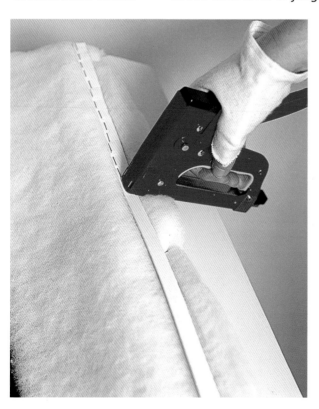

Stapling for a length of time by hand can cause blisters unless the hand is protected. A mitten, cut from a white cotton housework glove is an effective blister barrier.

When buying it, the salesman advised me never to use staples other than those intended for it. This I did until late one afternoon before a public holiday when I ran out and had to make do with the wrong brand of staples, purchased locally. I should have heeded the words of the oracle in the hardware store. The staple gun never worked properly again. Even when I did buy the correct staples, mostly they buckled up instead of going in. The former perfect action was never to return. The replacement (the same model exactly as the original) will never be loaded with the wrong staples.

Because mine is only a hand-operated staple gun, when using it I wear a cotton glove with the fingers cut out to avoid blisters developing between thumb and forefinger. It is also advisable to wear a glove when prising out tacks and staples with a screwdriver because the constant pressure of the handle on the palm also produces blisters.

A full-length apron with a large pocket protects clothes during all stages of upholstery and the pocket provides a safe receptacle for dislodged tacks and staples. In my experience, you invariably kick or knock over the container used for the ironmongery extracted when stripping a piece.

For easy access and to confer some sense of order on the kitchen, which is my preferred upholstery spot, I keep the tools I am using, as well as twine, tacks and staples, in a strong shopping basket.

The holder for my large upholstery needles is basic but effective; a piece of timber wrapped in fabric.

With the exceptions of a magnetised tack hammer, webbing stretcher, mallet, ripping chisel and upholstery needles, most tools for upholstery are commonplace and likely to be found in the average home workshop. It is always handy to keep a two pairs of scissors (one large, one small) with your upholstery tools.

Extensive repairs, involving accurate cutting of timber and the fitting, gluing and screwing of blocks to joints, were done to this chaise longue in an upholstery workshop.

REPAIRING CHAIR FRAMES

It is not difficult to identify a structural fault in a chair frame. Once a chair has been stripped you will be able to examine the frame. Splits in the timber can be easily repaired with good quality wood glue and clamped for 24 hours until completely dry.

Movement of any kind is a clear indication that all is not well and this usually happens at the joints. The joint may just need to be re-glued and clamped. If the damage is more extensive, you may need to call on the help of a cabinetmaker or furniture restorer. Sometimes dowel holes become enlarged and will have to be re-plugged and re-drilled and dowelled anew.

USEFUL TOOLS FOR THE HOME UPHOLSTERER

For Stripping Old Upholstery

- Screwdriver, pliers, mallet, ripping chisel, tack lifter (nail puller) for prising out and removing staples and tacks.
- Pincers, snips for removing or snipping off broken staples and tacks.
- Phillips head screwdrivers for removing swivel action pedestals and arms of office chairs.
- Allen keys, spanners – also for disassembling modern furniture.

For Mending Furniture

- Clamps for holding glued repairs steady while the glue dries.
- Rasp for removing sharp edges from inner rails and smoothing off roughened timber after stripping.

For Measuring and Marking

- Measuring tapes should be of cloth for sewing and retractable steel for measuring timber and furniture.
- Metal straightedge, at least 1 m (3¼ ft) as a minimum, 2 m (6½ ft) for preference, for drawing up cutting lines for piping as well as marking out covers. Or use a straight length of timber.
- Set square for determining accurate right angles and 45° angles.
- Removable marking pen or pencil for identifying upholstery pieces once fabric is cut out. Just to be sure, write on wrong side of fabric only.
- Seam gauge is a small ruler with a movable marker which takes the guesswork out of even hems and seams.

For Cutting

- Scissors – I have dressmaking scissors and so far they have cut through every fabric and hide I have used for upholstery.
- Rotary cutter and self-healing cutting board – not in my kit yet but people who have them are great enthusiasts. Excellent for cutting piping.
- Craft and trimming knives are useful for many cutting jobs. A sharp trimming knife with a flexible blade can be used to shave away and slope the ends of two strips of leather when making a lapped and glued join in piping (welting). Properly done, the join can barely be seen.

For Sewing

- Sewing machine – mine is a sturdy, ancient, domestic sewing machine which can even sew through leather without complaint. As well as forward and reverse, it does zigzag (buttonhole) stitch.
- Ironing equipment. A good quality pad and cover for the ironing board has been a minor but worthwhile investment. Mine is a basic steam and dry iron but I also keep a large spray bottle for water beside the ironing board. After being introduced to the wonders of hot iron cleaning preparation, I never have a burnt or sticking heat plate on the iron.

- Pins and needles are sewing's essentials. Discard any that catch when you insert them in your pin cushion or needle case; they are blunt and will pull threads and damage fabric. An emery bag attached to a pin cushion is recommended to keep pins and needles sharp. Don't wait until a needle breaks before replacing it; a new needle in the machine will make all the difference to the quality of stitching.
- Threads should be matched to fabrics if possible although polyester is used these days for practically everything. As well, have invisible (nylon) thread which can be used in machine or hand sewing and linen for hand sewing where strength is required.
- Stitch ripper (stitch unpicker) for unpicking seams. Buy the largest, sturdiest model, and for your convenience, have at least two in your sewing kit.
- A thimble protects the middle finger from needle pricks when hand sewing. For those who don't like the clammy feeling of wearing a thimble, there are flexible open-topped models.

For Upholstering

- Webbing stretcher is a simple tool used to tighten the loose end of a length of webbing prior to tacking it to a rail and is either pronged or in two parts with a bat and peg. You can easily make a wrap-around webbing stretcher from softwood, about the length of a felt-faced, blackboard duster. Wrap it in webbing (around its length) and use the angle between the outer edge of the chair rail opposite the first fixing and your piece of wood to catch the webbing before finally tightening it by exerting wrist pressure and tacking the end in place.
- Staple gun which takes 6 mm (¼ in) and 10 mm (⅜ in) staples. Buy the best you can afford and look after it.
- Tack hammer magnetised on one face. Some also have a nylon face which won't chip the finish on decorative upholstery nails. Or you can temporarily encase the striking face with a leather snood for 'soft' hammering jobs.
- Little skewers and heavy pins – although not yet in my possession, are good for temporarily anchoring fabrics on furniture. The 75 mm (3 in) skewers are also useful when machine sewing to stabilise fabric in front of the foot while keeping fingers well clear of the needle.
- Regulators are pointed at one end, round on the other and come in several lengths from 15 to 25 cm (6 to 10 in). They are poked through hessian (burlap) to adjust fibre fillings and stuffings, redistribute lumps and bring stuffing forward when stitching an edge roll on a seat. Although I have used a metal barbecue skewer for poking about in stuffing, I do not own a regulator.
- Upholstery needles are impressive for their size and variety. They can be curved or straight, pointed at both ends or at one end only, and some are up to 25 cm (10 in) long. Some have very big eyes for thick twine and cord.

FABRIC AND UPHOLSTERY MATERIALS

While choosing your fabric has the potential to be the most pleasant part of upholstering, it can often be a little daunting, with some people finding it very difficult indeed. A little preparation will help you narrow your choices for color and pattern and give you a starting point. With the immense ranges of beautiful fabrics available, there will always be something that will satisfy you.

Consider the color scheme in your room, and the decorating style. Do you want your newly upholstered piece to blend with other furnishings, or to stand out as the focal point of the room? Do you want the colors to contrast, or to complement those already there? Don't be intimidated by adding splashes of strong or unusual colors. Choosing a color you wouldn't normally surround yourself with can be enormously uplifting, as well as injecting new life into a tired environment.

Look at magazines for ideas on style, color, texture and pattern, and get a feel for what you like. Browse in decorating and homewares stores for ideas, then look around to see what fabrics are currently available. Don't restrict yourself to shopping only in fabric stores. Try seconds shops for remnants, homewares stores for bedspreads that are large enough for covering chairs, and shop at manufacturers who sell off-cuts. Although covering a couch may require a lot of fabric, it doesn't necessarily mean you have to spend a fortune on it.

Be sure you are making an economically sound purchase. If a chair has very little life left in it because it is poorly constructed from inferior materials, consider if it really is worth spending much on fabric. The most expensive cloth may not always be the one that will best serve your needs.

When choosing fabric, look for flexibility and strength, which affect durability; drape, which affects the finished appearance; and softness and absorbency, which will affect the comfort.

Be sure the fabric you are considering is suitable for the task you have in mind. It is exciting to be creative and break rules, but do this within reason. For example, covering a little-used chair in a glamorous sheer fabric is fun, frivolous and also very decorative. This same fine fabric may not be quite so suitable for a sofa that will be favoured by the family pet. Use color, pattern and texture to maximise the unexpected, rather than using a fragile, exotic fabric for effect alone.

If you find fabric you absolutely love, but which is a little too thin for the task, remember that a calico undercover, when tacked or stapled in place, will take the strain of the padding. The top cover fabric will be taut and smooth when stapled or tacked in place, but it will not be under such severe pressure. You could also try backing a curtain or dress-weight fabric

Left: Sheer covers permit an intriguing glimpse of the structure of these simple oak chairs.

with a fusible interfacing to make it stronger. Or, try a fusible wadding that will add extra padding as well. Fusible wadding on its own is great for making patterns – it tends to 'catch' on almost any surface and stay in place, making it easy to trace shapes directly onto it.

Consider the following when purchasing fabric:

- It is much easier if you choose a solid color or an all-over print that will not require matching. Stripes, checks and plaids will have to be matched. Small prints are easier to match than large prints.
- If fabric has design repeats, be sure they will work with the piece of furniture being covered. Measure repeats and check the measurements against the furniture you plan to cover.
- Texture is a great way to add design interest when using a single color. Take care to choose a fabric that won't snag.
- Be sure your machine can sew the fabric you are considering. Get advice about needles and thread for both lightweight and heavier fabrics, and for unusual fabrics. Fabrics with loops of thread on the wrong side may catch in the feed teeth of the machine, so you may have to place paper under the fabric to ensure it feeds smoothly.
- Look at fabric care instructions before buying. Will yours be easy to wash, or will it require dry cleaning, and how does this fit into your way of life?
- Check color-fastness to both light and water.

Firmly woven medium-weight fabrics work best for coverings, but don't let this inhibit your creativity. If you find a fabric that you think will be suitable, buy a small length and try it out. You may be surprised at how well it works. Purchase all the fabric you'll need from the one bolt where possible so there are no color variations.

Right: Manufacturers take much of the guesswork out of choosing fabrics by producing co-ordinated ranges of patterns and plains that are guaranteed to go together. Overleaf: Intense blue of a courtyard wall adjacent to a living area inspired the upholstery for these chairs.

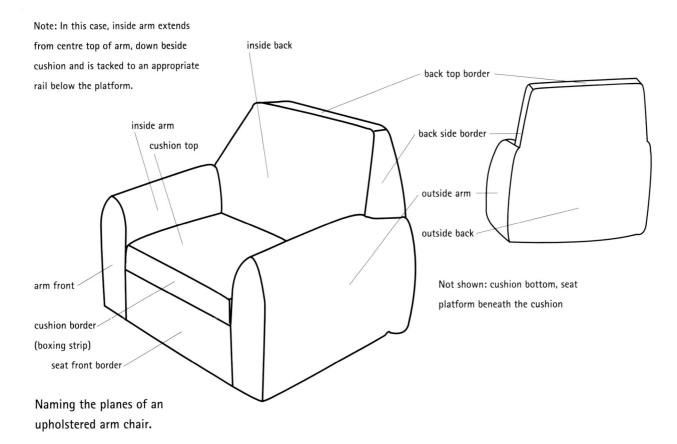

Note: In this case, inside arm extends from centre top of arm, down beside cushion and is tacked to an appropriate rail below the platform.

inside back

back top border

inside arm

back side border

cushion top

outside arm

outside back

arm front

Not shown: cushion bottom, seat platform beneath the cushion

cushion border (boxing strip)

seat front border

Naming the planes of an upholstered arm chair.

MEASURING FURNITURE FOR COVERING

Measure in inches or centimetres, don't mix the two. Where necessary, for ease of working and shopping (fabrics can only be bought in certain increments), some of the measurements have been rounded off, so they may not convert exactly. Use a fabric or fibreglass tape measure that will bend easily for measuring rounded areas. One with a hole in the end that can be pinned in place is helpful.

Make a sketch of the furniture item you plan to cover. Name the planes, such as the inside back, outside back, inside arm, outside arm, seat, seat border, and the arm facing. These are the most basic sections. The style of your furniture may combine two of these planes or even invent new ones.

Measure each plane individually as if you were cutting out the fabric for it. Measure the width first, as this will determine whether fabrics need to be joined, as may be the case for a sofa. With the inside back and inside arms of fully upholstered chairs, measure right down to where the lower edge is attached to the frame. Remember the old adage to measure twice and cut once. This will save unnecessary heartache later in the cutting and construction processes.

Use the old cover as a guide wherever possible but decide first if you want to make the padding on the piece thicker; more padding will mean more fabric. Undo the seams and lay the old cover on the new fabric as a pattern. You may need to add to the seam allowances; any excess can be trimmed away later.

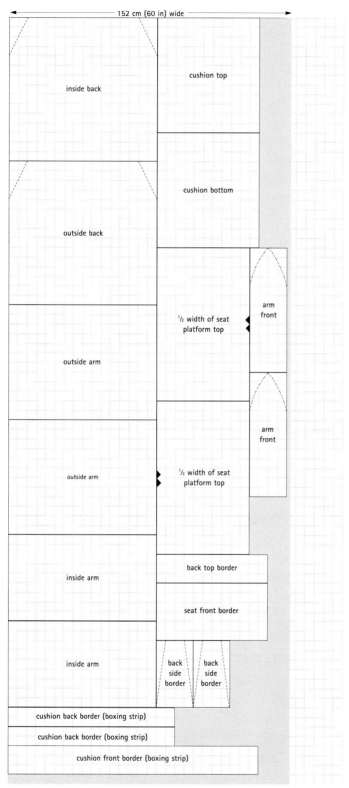

152 cm (60 in) wide

inside back

cushion top

cushion bottom

outside back

outside arm

arm front

½ width of seat platform top

outside arm

arm front

½ width of seat platform top

inside arm

back top border

seat front border

inside arm

back side border

back side border

cushion back border (boxing strip)

cushion back border (boxing strip)

cushion front border (boxing strip)

1 square = 5 cm (2 in)

4 m (4½ yd) of 152 cm (60 in) wide plain fabric is required to upholster the arm chair opposite. To economise, seat platform is cut in two pieces and joined. Cushion back border accommodates zipper.

ESTIMATING THE AMOUNT OF FABRIC NEEDED

Where planes are irregular shapes, it is best to treat them as rectangles using the largest length and width measurements. You will trim the piece to fit when it is being fitted on the chair or stitched in the case of cushions and loose covers.

Draw the planes to scale on graph paper adding 5 cm (2 in) all around for seams. When estimating for loose covers where no loose cover exists, add a 10 - 20 cm (4 - 8 in) tuck-in to each piece at the back of seats and sides of seats. Remember to add length for hems, and allow for a skirt (valance) if desired. For gathered skirts, multiply the circumference of the chair by two and a half. Don't forget to mark each cushion as well.

If you plan to use piping made from the same fabric, make a pattern for this as well. You cannot always cut piping from scraps. Piping for loose cushions is cut on the cross; piping which is tacked or stapled to a frame is cut straight.

Cut out the paper pieces. Use another piece of graph paper to represent your fabric width and place the upholstery pieces on the fabric paper. Most upholstery and furnishing fabrics are 137 cm (54 in) or 152 cm (60 in) wide. Mark any fabric pattern repeats on the fabric graph paper and on the pieces of upholstery graph paper. Allow for the grain and any one-way design or nap requirements. Trace around shapes or glue cut outs onto fabric graph paper.

Piece fabric for large furniture, such as sofas, at the sides, with a full width running down the centre. When joining, keep seams as unobtrusive as possible and away from areas of wear and tear. If it is necessary to join in the centre, add piping and make a design detail of the join.

Railroading fabric can help to save time and fabric when making covers for sofas. Instead of running fabric from back to front, running it from side to side eliminates the need for joins and may be more economical. This will not work with one-way or nap designs. Railroading may compromise the life of the cover as the stronger warp threads of the fabric are not running in the direction of the greatest wear.

Be generous when estimating – extra fabric can always be used for cushions or other decorative accents, but if you don't have enough fabric, you may not be able to get more.

In time, you may be able to do all these graph paper calculations either in your head or perhaps with the help of pencil and paper.

Above: Upholstered pelmet disguises the curtain tops and adds distinction to the window. Railroading the pelmet piece would have been uneconomical so the fabric was joined with a excellent pattern match on the left-hand side. Opposite: Woven chevron-style stripes in a sturdy Indian cotton run down this upholstered chair from top of inside back to the seat front and require little wasteful pattern-matching.

MARKING PATTERNS ONTO FABRIC

For loose covers, prewash cotton fabric to allow shrinkage to take place. Always press all fabrics before cutting out. Trim the selvedges so they don't cause seam puckering.

If the cover you are making is very tailored and you have any uncertainties about fit, make it up in calico (muslin) first before cutting into expensive fabric. Make any necessary adjustments on the calico, then use it as a pattern for cutting out.

Mark pattern pieces directly onto the right side of your fabric with tailor's chalk or a disappearing marker (one that is air soluble), or pin any paper patterns in place. Mark all pieces on the fabric before you begin cutting, including any amounts needed for piping. If the pieces don't all fit the first time, try rearranging them until they do.

If your fabric has motifs or design repeats, they will need to be placed the right way up and/or centred. If you are marking pattern pieces directly onto your fabric with a marker, this is easy. If you cut from a pattern, cut away the central area of the pattern so it's easy to see the fabric. Centre motifs on the seat, the back, and on each arm if applicable.

CUTTING

Use large, sharp dressmaking shears, or a rotary cutter and cutting mat. Cut out on a large section of clean floor, or a very large cutting table. Don't have excess fabric hanging over the edge of a table as this stretches it out of shape, and certain pieces can end up being shorter than you intended.

After cutting fabric, mark the top and bottom and centres of each piece with a disappearing marker in the seam allowance.

MATERIALS

Timber is the traditional material use for the frames of chairs, sofas and stools. However, iron was used for the backs and arms of some Victorian chairs where stitching has to be employed to fasten paddings and fabrics instead of tacks or staples.

Today, you are likely to encounter all kinds of materials in furniture. Legs can be stainless steel, iron or even aluminium. Molded plastic frequently forms the backs of office chairs. A side panel of an executive chair may be moulded plastic for the inside arm and armrest with an external face of hardboard. A bed head may be medium-density fibreboard (MDF) or particleboard. A seat and back of a chair may be formed in one piece from plywood. Plastic, hardboard, MDF, particleboard and ply can all be stapled with surprising ease, although on corners and places which are host to many staples, sometimes the fibrous materials such as hardboard and particleboard start to break down. Fortunately, you can usually find somewhere in the near vicinity to drive in your staples.

In the sitting position, 90% of the body's weight is assigned to the seat which is why its construction and padding must be sturdy. The traditional foundation is an interlaced webbing of jute or linen supporting coiled springs over which padding is placed. Or the seat support could be provided by rubber webbing, arched zigzag springs or a grid of metal or fabric straps attached to closely wound coil springs – which are in turn fastened to the inner faces of the front, back and side rails. With these more modern support systems, foam is usually the material chosen for cushioning. It is convenient and easy to use but not as long lasting as curled hair and fibre which can be re-used time after time. The higher quality foams have a maximum guaranteed life of ten years although, when only lightly used, they can last many more years.

Tacks or Staples?

The traditional fixing for webbing and fabric to timber frames is done with tacks. One type of tack hammer has a magnetised face which is used to pick up tacks and save your fingers from being pricked. The unmagnetised face is used for striking the tack into the timber frame. A slip tack is only driven in half way and is a temporary method of fixing. It is removed with a clawed tack lifter, pliers, or by striking it a glancing blow with the tack hammer. After being hammered a tack becomes bent and blunt so cannot be used a second time. Sizes range from 6 mm (¼ in) to 25 mm (1 in).

As a fixing method, staples require much less skill than tacks. With an air-powered staple gun, fixing can be done at great speed and with minimum effort. Supporters of stapling are quick to point out that staples make less of an impression on timber than tacks, which leave quite large holes. When tack holes are densely clumped together they can contribute to splits in the chair frame. The most commonly used sizes of staple in upholstery are 6 mm (¼ in) and 10 mm (⅜ in).

Personal preference and skill levels will determine which method is selected.

Webbing

Tightly stretched webbing makes a foundation for coiled springs or spring-less padding. The most common and inexpensive type is made from jute. More costly versions are elasticised or made from canvas, linen or rubber.

Hessian (Burlap)

Strong, inexpensive, coarsely woven fabric used over webbing and springs.

Curled Horse Hair

The preferred stuffing for antiques and the best custom-made pieces, curled horse hair has become expensive and difficult to obtain (see page 40). The curled hair from cattle tails is considered to be a satisfactory substitute.

Coir Fibre

Taken from the outer covering of the coconut, it is used as a substitute for horse hair and is particularly useful for insulating coiled springs and disguising the depressions between them, and as a base for soft paddings.

Polyurethane Foam

In modern furniture manufacturing, this material has replaced fibre fillings and is available in densities ranging from extra soft through to extra firm, and in many different thicknesses, from 5 mm to 10 cm (¼ in to 4 in). Can be cut with an electric carving knife but it is preferable to ask your supplier to cut it for you. Always use fire-resistant foam.

Flocking

Soft, fluffy by-product of the garment industry. It is picked over and teased out by hand and placed, a handful at a time, on a hessian foundation to form a layer of padding.

Linters

This loosely felted raw cotton comes in a roll and is used as an even layer of soft padding under a calico (muslin) cover.

Polyester Filling

Most commonly seen in small packs as a white toy filling, although it is much more economical to purchase it in greater quantity (in white or grey crimped fleecy form) for upholstery.

Polyester Wadding (Batting)

Sold by the metre (yard) or in rolls and is a good, stable, easy-to-handle padding material. It is mainly used to provide a comfortable layer of padding between foam and the top cover fabric.

Fusible (Iron-on) Wadding
A very a thin version of polyester wadding with heat-activated glue on one side. Available from craft and sewing supply stores, it is ideal for adding a little extra bulk to fabrics which may be insufficiently sturdy for upholstery.

Twine
Jute or cotton twine is used to attach springs to webbing and when hand stitching into hessian (burlap) is required.

Laidcord
Heavy duty cord, usually of man-made fibre, used for tying down springs.

Coiled Springs
Available in sizes ranging from 10 - 30 cm (4 - 12 in) and in different gauges (thinner for backs, thicker for seats).

Calico (Muslin)
Available in various widths and in different weights. Unbleached is the least expensive and is most often used to cover padding for traditional upholstery.

Back Tacking Strips
Long, thin strips of cardboard used to reinforce and neaten the edge of a cover; especially effective against piping. Also used when stapling or tacking an edge roll onto a chair rail.

Ready-made Edge Roll
Usually made from a paper-like substance with a flange, it provides a softer edge for seats and also constrains seat padding material.

Flexible Metal Tacking Strip
Also known as shark's teeth and hide-a-tack, flexible metal tacking strip comes in a coil and is used instead of blind stitching on outside back covers. Only suited to fairly heavy fabrics.

Gimp Pins
Small tacks with fine heads in various colors, used beneath decorative upholstery nails and to attach trims.

Upholstery Nails
Seams and joins of leather chairs are often closely studded with decorative upholstery nails. Available in a variety of head shapes, sizes and colors.

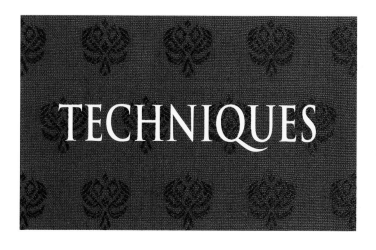

TECHNIQUES

The materials and methods which have become the vocabulary of upholstery were born of necessity. The materials were chosen because they were the cheapest, most accessible and most appropriate for the job. The methods used were the most efficient ways of completing the best job in the shortest possible time. This does not mean to say that padding has to be covered with calico (muslin) if you have something else suitable on hand. Or that a knot or stitch of your own invention will hold any less well than those set down in the upholsterer's guidebook.

Here are some basics to peruse. No doubt, you will indulge in a little resourceful method-making of your own when you are in the throes of an upholstery project.

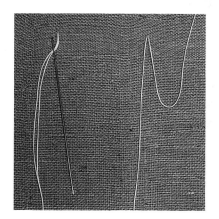
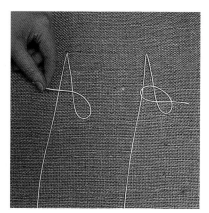

SLIP KNOT

The slip knot always involves two lengths of string with the right looped and knotted around the left. The example shown here is a single slip knot which is suitable for most upholstery jobs. Where great strain is to be exerted on the knot, it is doubled by winding the right string around twice before feeding it through the loop which forms the knot. The more you pull a slip knot the tighter it becomes. Secure it with a hitch knot (last step on right) which locks off the 'play' of the left string.

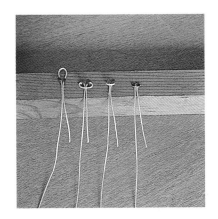

TACKING DOWN TWINE

When tying down springs, the twine has to be attached securely to the seat rail. You could use staples (do it twice, the second time like a back stitch over four strings) although sometimes the twine is severed by the staples. Or use the double tack method as shown on the left. Slip tack the pair of tacks close together. Pass a loop of twine between them and up over both tack heads, then drive in the tacks.

CLOVE HITCH KNOT FOR LASHING SPRINGS

Springs are mostly tied to one another and then attached to the seat rails so their top coils are directly in line with their bottom coils. With dining chairs, top coils are sometimes sloped slightly towards the centre. A good method of lashing springs together evenly is to start at the centre and work out to the rails. The clove hitch knot photographed at left is well suited to the tying of springs because it will not loosen in a chain reaction if the twine breaks at one point.

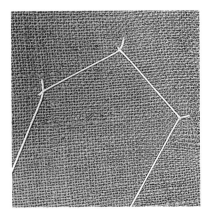

SEWING SPRINGS TO HESSIAN

Using a curved needle and twine, fasten the spring to hessian with three stitches looped around the top coil. Use the same method for attaching springs to webbing.

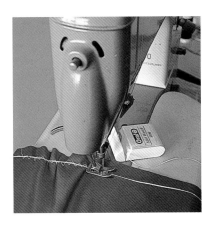

GATHERING OVER DENTAL FLOSS

When gathering medium to heavyweight fabrics or long lengths, use machine zigzag stitch over dental floss. Make sure that the machine stitch clears the dental floss. This is a time-saving gathering technique which always gives an even result.

MAKING CONTINUOUS PIPING

Use this method when you need to make large amounts of piping. It is easier than joining many strips together.

Step 1 Make a square of fabric by folding the cut edge of the fabric diagonally to match a selvedge edge. Cut out along the remaining selvedge.

Step 2 Press the fabric square in half diagonally, taking care not to stretch the fabric. Cut along the pressed line.

Step 3 Pin straight edges together and stitch with a 6 mm (¼ in) seam allowance to form a parallelogram (a rectangle on a slope).

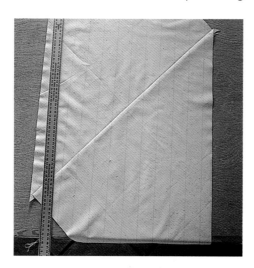

Step 4 With tailor's chalk, mark parallel lines on the fabric, from raw edge to raw edge. For narrow piping, mark them about 4 cm (1½ in) apart.

Step 5 With right sides together, match the short edges to form a tube. Slide the fabric so that one marked width extends beyond the edge. Stitch together with a 6 mm (¼ in) seam, then press the seam open.

Step 6 Turn the tube right side out. With scissors, cut along the marked line to make a continuous strip of bias fabric. Another cutting method is to unthread the needle thread on an overlocker (serger), and line up the marked line with the cutting blade. The needle will pierce the fabric in the seam allowance, while the cutting blade will cut a continuous strip of fabric.

Step 7 Fold the fabric strip in half with the wrong sides together. Place the piping cord in the fold. Keeping the edges together, with a zipper foot, stitch close to the cord.

MAKING CUSHION COVERS

Rounded or tapered corners make cushion corners appear more graceful, and it is easier to add piping or other trims to them.

Step 1 Cut two squares 2 cm (¾ in) larger than the cushion size.

Step 2 Fold each square into quarters, matching all raw edges, and pin to hold.

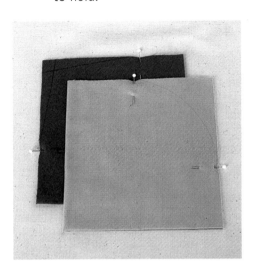

Step 3 To make rounded corners, place a plate on the corner and trace around it with a disappearing marker. To make tapered corners, measure and mark 2 cm (¾ in) from the corner, then another 10 cm (4 in) from the two corners. Connect the points with a straight line as shown.

Step 4 Stitch together with a 1 cm (⅜ in) seam, leaving an opening in one side. Zigzag close to the stitching. Trim the excess seam allowance.

Step 5 Turn right side out and press. Place a cushion insert in the cover, or stuff with fibre fill. Slip stitch the opening closed.

CHAIRS

New padding, a buttoned seat and fresh fabric transform an old wrought iron telephone chair.

The old foam seat pad was supported by a circular piece of timber drilled with holes for air vents. These holes inspired a pattern for tufting and buttoning; a technique which was originally devised to anchor loose padding material but used here in a purely decorative manner. By adding a total of four more holes, the first three appeared more evenly spaced. The fault was not evident until the seat was padded and tufted – at which point the padding had to be unfastened to make more holes and corresponding slits in the foam.

A small star motif from the seat fabric was enlarged on a photocopier, cut out in yellow fabric and fused to the inside back of the chair.

MATERIALS

Print fabric and two
co-ordinating plain fabrics

Calico (muslin)

Medium density seat foam
50 mm (2 in) thick

Thick polyester
wadding (batting)

Twine

7 self-cover buttons
15 mm (⅝ in) diameter

8 self-cover buttons
13 mm (½ in) diameter

Paper-backed fusible web

Fusible wadding (batting)

Fusible interfacing

Matching sewing thread

Scissors

Power drill with
13 mm (½ in) bit

Upholstery needle
10 cm (4 in) long

7 dowelling plugs or
improvised equivalents

Staple gun

Tape measure

Brown paper

Disappearing fabric marker

To paint the wrought iron, a three-sided (two sides and a bottom) spray booth was taped together from flattened cardboard boxes and the spraying was done outdoors. The right color was not available in one can so cream and bright yellow were combined. By lightly misting one color over the other and allowing drying time in between, the right shade appeared.

Removing tacks from the underside of the seat.

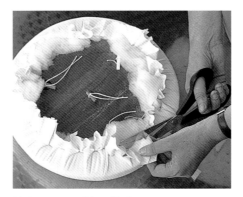

Twine secured by slip knots over cut lengths of pencil and chopstick.

After realising buttons were unequally spaced, padding fastening was removed and more holes drilled.

MAKING A PATTERN

Remove the existing chair covers. If possible, use these pieces as patterns for the new cover.

Inside back Tape paper to the inside back of chair. Fold it loosely around the edges to the outside back. Trace the outline about 2.5 cm (1 in) from the outside back edges. Add 1.5 cm (⅝ in) to all edges for seams and 3 cm (1¼ in) to the lower edge for a hem. Using a photocopier, enlarge a motif from the fabric or another source, to fit the inside back of chair.

Outside back Pin the inside back pattern to the chair. Tape paper to the outside back and fold it to make a pattern to cover it, lapping over the inside back edges by about 12 mm (½ in). Add seam and hem allowances as for the inside back, then cut out. Cut the pattern in half lengthwise.

Seat Depressions made by drawing down the buttons require more fabric than a smooth cover. The plain undercover will give a guide to the eventual amount required. Measure the circle of calico prior to upholstering, then measure the amount trimmed away after stapling; the difference between these two will give the size for the cover fabric.

CUTTING OUT

From one co-ordinating color, cut an inside back and two outside backs (one from each pattern piece), adding 5 cm (2 in) to the centres of the outside backs for facings. Cut a back placket the length of the chair's outside back by 10 cm (4 in).

From fusible wadding, cut an inside back. From fusible interfacing, cut two outside backs and a placket.

ASSEMBLING

Applying the Motif

With a pencil, trace the photocopied motif onto the paper side of the fusible web. Following the manufacturer's instructions, fuse the web to the wrong side of the second co-ordinating fabric and cut out the pieces. With a disappearing fabric marker, trace the motif from the photocopy onto the centre of the inside back. You may need to tape the paper, then the fabric to a lightbox or a window to do this. Remove the paper backing from the motif and fuse the pieces in place on the inside back, using the tracing as a placement guide.

Cutting out the enlarged motif which has been fused to the wrong side of the yellow fabric.

Ironing the motif to the background fabric for the inside back of chair.

Making the Outside Back

Fuse the interfacing to the outside backs and to the placket. Narrow hem the centre back edges. Fold 2 cm (¾ in) to the wrong side at the centre backs for facings. Mark and stitch eight evenly spaced buttonholes to fit the smaller buttons. Place the centre backs face down, next to each other. Place the placket over them, face down, aligning tops and bottoms. Baste the placket in place in the seam allowance at the upper edge. Press the seam allowances to the wrong side around the top and sides.

Buttons are sewn to the placket for the back opening.

Joining the Back

Fuse the wadding to the wrong side of the inside back. Place the inside back on the chair, pressing the edges over the sides. Place the outside back on the chair, pinning it to the inside back. Gather or pleat the upper corners of the inside back. Remove the cover and topstitch the outside back in place. Hem the lower edge. Cover the buttons following the manufacturer's instructions and sew them on the placket to match the buttonholes.

Seat

Strip the old cover and padding. Drill evenly spaced holes in timber for buttoning. Mark corresponding points on foam and make slits through these points with scissors. Cut circle of wadding at least 30 cm (12 in) larger overall than the base.

Place foam over seat, aligning drilled holes with slits in foam. Place circle of wadding and a generously cut circle of calico over the foam. Measure diameter of the calico circle.

Thread upholstery needle with 50 cm (20 in) of twine and insert to one side of the centre hole drilled in the underside of the seat, through all layers, leaving at least 15 cm (6 in) of twine trailing. Return the needle to the other side of the centre hole catching a little scrap of calico in the loop of the stitch on top. Remove needle from twine and tie a slip knot (see page 65) over a dowelling plug (or similar) spanning the hole, pulling the calico and padding down to form a hollow. Stitch and slip knot remaining drilled holes in the same way. When satisfied that all tufted hollows are the same depth, remove dowelling plugs and while holding twine ends firmly, staple twice (the second time to fold twine back on itself) beside drilled holes.

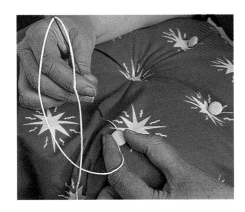

Buttoning the top fabric using twine and upholstery needle.

Smooth wadding and calico to the underside of the seat. Staple wadding to the timber in at least eight equidistant points. Arrange calico evenly on the underside making pleats radiating from the depressions in the padding where necessary. Staple calico to the timber, starting on opposite sides first at four equidistant points and firmly pulling at the calico before stapling to ensure a smooth result. Trim excess fabric and calico.

Cover the seven larger buttons following manufacturer's instructions. Cut cover fabric to size (see above) and apply it to the seat from the centre with twine and needle using buttons instead of fabric squares on top and stapling the twine ends twice on the underside. Smooth fabric to the underside, pulling firmly. Before stapling to the timber, pleat the excess from the buttons where necessary. Trim away the surplus fabric.

DINING CHAIR with SPRUNG SEAT

Bought as one of a set of six from a second-hand furniture dealer who boasted openly that he alone had done all the re-upholstering, this chair's seat was both uncomfortable and unsightly, as were all the others. Apart from insufficient anchoring of springs and stuffing, instead of being calico the undercover was a fleecy-lined stretch fabric which encouraged 'give' where 'control' was required.

As is often the case with sprung dining chairs, the springs were very tall. Perhaps I should have bought new, shorter springs but the originals seemed to be sound when tested. Check springs on a flat surface by pushing each one down over itself; those that lean to one side should be discarded.

To reduce spring height it is possible to bend back the end coils but this means that only the most rigid part of the spring, the middle section, bears

MATERIALS

Webbing, 5 cm (2 in) wide
Webbing stretcher
Scissors
Curved needle
Staple gun
Twine
Laidcord (spring twine)
Hessian (burlap)
Ready-made edge roll
Cardboard back tacking strips
Cotton flocking
Coir fibre
Double-pointed upholstery needle
Polyester fibrefill
Calico (muslin)
Leather
Tack hammer
Gimp pins
Brass-headed upholstery nails

Above: In its original state this seat was a comfort-free zone.
Right: Finished chair covered in leather with a triangular pattern of ten brass-headed upholstery nails at both front corners.

the load. A spring's flexibility is contained in its end coils because they are larger and therefore more elastic than the spring's stiffer 'waist'.

To build up the edge, contain the stuffing and create a slight overhang which will give the chair a generously padded look I used a flanged paper edge roll. This is an easier alternative to a stitched edge roll which is formed by dragging the stuffing held beneath hessian to the edge with a regulator before securing it, in a ridge, with rows of stitching.

To ensure all chairs in a matched set are equally padded, calculate the weight of each type of stuffing on the first chair. Start with a kilo (or approximately two pounds) of whatever first stuffing you are using, then weigh what is left when you have finished. Subtract this from the original amount and you have the correct quantity for the next chair. Proceed in this manner with other stuffings.

There is a fair bit of stretching and cajoling of the leather at the front corners in order to make neat pleats. When dampened with a cloth, the leather quickly becomes flexible and what seems like an impossible task at the outset can soon be achieved.

1 Padding and undercover were descending through webbing.

2 Stapling webbing to side rails. Use both ends of webbing roll to stretch two strips at once.

STRIPPING

Strip covers and all upholstery from chair, cutting springs away with a craft knife. If springs do not stand straight and even after being pressed down on themselves or if they sway and deform when being pressed, discard and buy new ones. Reserve cover; it will serve as a pattern when buying and cutting leather.

WEBBING AND SPRINGS

Webbing for a chair with springs is attached to the underside of the frame. Measure and mark positions of each strip on the chair frame before you start, allowing a little less space than the width of the webbing between each one. Note that because of the seat shape, the webbing will fan out from the back to the front.

Undo webbing roll from the centre and outside and work from both ends. With the chair up-ended on a table and the back hanging over the table's edge, it is convenient to start anchoring two strips of webbing with staples at the front and then to stretch and staple them to the back rail. At the front, staple into 2.5 cm (1 in) turned up hems, offsetting or angling the staples for maximum grip in the timber. Using the stretching tool as a lever, stretch the webbing until it pings when flicked with the forefinger. Then staple taut webbing at least three times into back rail, cut webbing from roll (allowing hem turn up) and staple the flap back. Finish all front-to-back strips before inter-weaving, stretching and attaching webbing across the seat.

Turn the chair right side up and arrange springs on top of the webbing so they are equally spaced from one another (never more

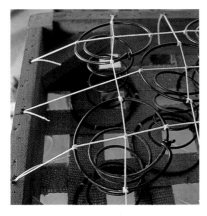

3 Springs are lashed to one another then attached to the rails using the double-tack method.

4 Hessian cover is stapled over the springs, corners mitred and the flaps turned towards the centre.

5 Ready-made edge roll is stapled to seat edge. Back tacking strip over the flange evenly distributes the load making the fixing more secure.

than 10 cm or 4 in apart), preferably at webbing cross points so that stitching the springs also anchors the webbing and with top joins angled slightly to the centre. Keep springs well forward in the seat (about 6.5 cm or 2½ in from front rail) as this is where most of the load will be borne. Mark positions of springs on webbing before stitching them to webbing using the same method as 'Sewing Springs to Hessian' on page 66.

Working from the centre out with lengths of laidcord at least twice the width of the seat, lash the springs to one another on their top coils using the clove hitch knot described on page 66.

Because I wanted to shorten the springs, I depressed them all by 4 cm (1½ in) using a bread board lashed to the chair seat with a luggage strap. I gauged the amount of extra pressure required to incline the outer coils in order to make a slightly rounded seat shape, pulled on the cords as necessary and fastened them all to the chair rails using the double tack method for tacking down twine described on page 66.

COVERING SPRINGS

A cover of hessian over the springs prevents padding material dropping down to the webbing. Cut hessian at least 10 cm (4 in) larger all around than the seat. (Take note of the size and add a further 13 cm (5 in) all around for the calico undercover.) Centre hessian over seat and staple it to the centre of the back rail, then draw it tightly over the springs and staple to the centre of the front rail. Staple to centres of side rails, pulling hessian tight. Then fasten from centres to corners, pulling hessian firmly before stapling. At inner corners of the back posts, fold the points of the hessian towards the centre of the seat and slash diagonally from these points to the corners of the back posts. Now the fabric can be stapled from here to the back and side rails without obstruction. Trim hessian to 2.5 cm (1 in) beyond seat line and finger press the excess towards the centre.

EDGE ROLL

Allowing one third of its width to overhang the seat, staple ready-made edge roll to seat with back tacking strip over the flange to hold it firmly in place. Start at the back with the cut end of the roll abutting the back post. To turn each corner neatly, cut a wedge-shaped mitre in the flange of the roll prior to stapling. Just before finishing at the other back post, cut edge roll to fit. Measure, cut and staple edge roll with back tacking strip to back rail.

6 So the springs stay securely in position, their tops have been sewn to the hessian.

7 Cotton flocking pads out the edge while stitched–down coir fibre insulates the springs.

8 A little extra flocking pads out the indentations formed by stitching the coir fibre.

9 A 'cloud' of polyester fibrefill, the final padding here, will be constrained by calico.

10 Calico cover is stapled midway on the outer faces of the rails. Back corner flaps are tucked between back posts and stuffing.

PADDING

Secure hessian to spring tops using twine and a curved needle; see 'Sewing Springs to Hessian' page 66.

Tease out then pack cotton flocking in the hollow inside the edge roll. Each handful is kneaded with those already in place so the padding becomes even and well blended. Then arrange sufficient coir fibre over the centre of the seat to insulate the tops of the springs. With a long double-pointed upholstery needle, stitch the coir fibre to the hessian (avoiding the springs and the webbing beneath them) with long stitches in a cross formation.

Tease out and add more flocking over the indentations caused by the stitching.

Place polyester fibrefill on top of the flocking and coir padding, teasing it to avoid lumps and voids. Although the amount seems impossibly high, it condenses to quite a slim layer.

Cut calico cover 13 cm (5 in) larger all around than the hessian spring cover. Centre calico on seat and staple it to the centre of the outside face of the back rail. Pulling on calico firmly to pack down filling, staple it to the centre outside face of front rail. Similarly, staple calico to the sides. Then fasten from centres to corners, dragging down calico firmly before stapling. At the front corners, gather and staple excess calico forcefully. At inner corners of the back posts, slash calico diagonally so fabric can be taken without obstruction to the back and side rails. The flaps formed by the slashes are pushed into the crevices between the stuffing and the back posts.

COVER

Examine leather for flaws and using the original cover as a guide, determine the best way to cut into the hide. In order to avoid defects and blemishes, the cover was pieced with a join at the back and the seam sewn with ordinary thread and needle on the sewing machine.

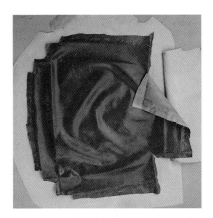

11 Using the old cover as a rough pattern for the new. Back is pieced to avoid flaws in hide.

12 Positioning cover on chair to determine slashing for leather to fit around the back posts.

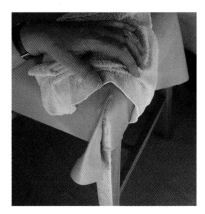

13 Stretching and stapling to form corner pleat. Damp cloth increases flexibility of leather.

Aligning the back seam with the inner corners of the back posts and stretching the leather, staple the back and front to the centre points of the underside of the back and front rails respectively. Staple gradually to within 10 cm (4 in) of the corners, stretching as you go. Then staple the sides of the cover under the side rails working from opposite centres to within 10 cm (4 in) of the corners.

Fold leather forward at the inner corners of the back posts and slash diagonally and fix to undersides of side and back rails following method for calico undercover.

Make leather pliable at the front corners by moistening it with a damp cloth. When the leather is sufficiently stretched to make a neat corner pleat which molds nicely to the shape of the seat padding, staple cover under the seat, up to the outside face of the front leg. Snip leather to release it from beneath the seat and trim the piece which will travel across the outside leg so it has a narrow turn-up. Pull this side piece forward, turning under the 'hem' and staple it to the front face of the leg. Trim away excess beyond the corner staples carefully calculating what needs to remain when the pleat is closed over. Staple cover under seat, up to front face of the front leg and snip to release leather as for outside face of leg. Gauge the depth for the front leg turn-up and mitre corner leaving just sufficient at the corner to barely turn under the raw edge.

Having decided on a pattern for upholstery nails, use a few gimp pins to secure the pleats on the front faces ensuring that front and side 'hems' and corners are turned under. Place gimp pins just a pin head away from the proposed positions of the upholstery nails as the nails will cover them.

Before driving in the upholstery nails, muffle one face of the tack hammer with leather so as not to scuff the nail heads.

Trim away excess leather from beneath chair.

Cover the underside with calico, turning hems under before stapling.

COVERING an ARMCHAIR

Purchased inexpensively from a warehouse where it had languished for years, this rather handsome, old-fashioned chair was in good shape with springs and padding in excellent condition. Most probably prepared for a slipcover when last upholstered, its undercover of very fine, scrim-like calico (muslin) was soiled and dusty. Although removing most of the calico did not disturb the padding beneath, it did yield accurate pattern pieces from which a new, fitted cover could be cut.

I used a length of seven metres (eight yards) of 120 cm (48 in) wide fabric for this chair and when finished I had barely a metre over. The indents formed by the padding and the crevices leading to the rails where arm, seat and inside back pieces are attached all greedily consumed fabric.

A great advantage of working with striped fabric is that the straight grain of the fabric is always glaringly obvious; distortion and unevenness result if upholstery pieces are not cut on the straight grain of fabric. Stripes are also very simple to pattern-match and they can be centred easily on the chair.

Adhering to the correct work sequence is crucial for the success of any upholstery project. A logical order is revealed when removing the old cover. Reverse this stripping order when applying the new cover.

To avoid unwanted gathers or fullness when stapling fabric, work from the centre point to the edges, smoothing the fabric out as you proceed.

Use short staples (6 mm or ¼ in) when attaching fabric to timber and the longer staples (10 mm or ⅜ in) to go through cardboard back-tacking strips and padding as well as fabric. If the staples don't connect, try tapping them with a hammer.

There are similarities between upholstery and sewing. You frequently fasten two pieces of fabric together with the right sides together and raw edges matching – just like sewing a seam. After fastening the top of the outside back, it becomes impossible to work in this way and methods for concealing any fastenings directly applied to the right side of the fabric have to be devised. Here, the staples were covered by gimp (upholstery braid) which was glued and pinned in place.

Opposite: The armchair resplendent in its new striped cover.
Inset: The first front panel on the arm has been removed.

STRIPPING

Prior to removing pieces of the old cover, write a code on the timber frame indicating the piece of fabric attached to it, such as TOB for top of outside

1 Stripping continues with outside arms, outside back and back border removed.

2 Centre line marked on inside back and corner section extended with newspaper.

back. Strip away old cover, noting the stripping order and labelling the pieces to correspond with codes on the frame. With chairs of this type, start with the front arm panels, then the outside back and outside arms before stripping the inside sections.

In this case, undercover fabric was left on the rectangular front arm panels because it was easy to calculate and cut new fabric for these pieces. Beside these panels, the side front posts were also left intact. Some of the cardboard back-tacking strips were salvaged and labeled. All the old tacks and staples not engaged in fastening the remaining upholstery were removed from the frame using pliers and screwdriver.

Retrieved undercover pieces were pressed and where appropriate, their centre lines indicated with marking pen. The inside back piece was asymmetrical at its lower edge so it was evened out with newspaper. Slashes to allow the fabric to encircle frame uprights and joins were noted.

In the stripping process the hessian and cotton wadding (batting) had to be removed from the outside arms, outside back, back border (between the inside back and outside back) and the lower seat front border. All these pieces were reserved and labeled ready to be used again. When re-applied, the hessian went on first with seam allowance turned under and stapling starting on opposite sides and working out to the corners. Then the wadding was anchored beneath the first back tacking strip when each piece of cover fabric was stapled on.

CUTTING OUT

New fabric was cut with a view to matching the stripes in all but the back border piece, which was deliberately cut the other way with stripes running parallel to its long sides. Slashes in the lower sides on the inside back (so fabric can 'straddle' posts) were transferred to the fabric in marking pen but not cut at this stage.

3 Fixing the inside back to the top rail with staples.

4 Arm pieces pushed through seat crevice prior to stapling.

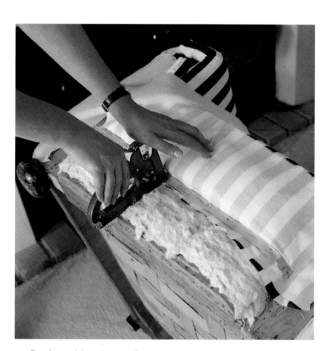

5 Back tacking lower front border.

COVERING

Matching the centre of the inside back on the fabric to the same centre point on the frame, the fabric was stapled to the frame, working from the mid point out.

Arms were positioned and their lower edges pushed down beside the seat. The lower edge of the inside back was also pushed down the back seat crevice. The chair was turned upside down in order to staple the arms to the underside of the arm rails. With the fabric pulled taut, stapling continued around to the front arm via the side front posts (uprights). Then the lower edges of the arms were stapled to their designated rails with slashes made where necessary so fabric could be wrapped around any obstructing rails, posts and joins.

The seat and the front border beneath the seat were machine stitched (right sides together) with piping cord between them. Using a curved needle, the resulting seam allowance was backstitched to the appropriate indent at the front of the chair. Then the back of the seat was pushed through the back seat crevice, pulled tight and stapled in place. The lower edge of the front border was stapled to its rail.

The lower front border was stapled in place over its backing of hessian and cotton padding using a tacking strip to even out the stress on the cover fabric and create a neat fold line. To pad this section further, a layer

6 Lower edges of inside back are slashed to accommodate obstructing members of the chair and stapled to appropriate rails and posts.

of polyester wadding was set over the cotton padding before the lower edge was stapled to the underside of the chair. Then the sides of this piece were stapled to the arm fronts.

The back border with its back-tacking strip was attached by starting from the centre point and working down to the arms. More wadding was positioned over the original padding, the back border folded right way up and the junction at the arms folded in to conceal the raw edges. Then the other long raw edge of this piece was stapled to the top rail and to the side posts of the outside back.

At this stage, the lower edge of the inside back was stapled to the outside back of the chair with slashes made where necessary so fabric could be wrapped around rails, posts and joins that were in the way.

Back-tacking strips were cut for the front and top edges of the outside arm pieces. Hessian was attached and padding positioned on the outside arms. Front edges were back tacked then the fabric folded right way up and three staples applied to hold the opposite side to the outside back. Then a back-tacking strip was folded into the seam allowance of the upper edge and the piece 'top-stitched' with staples at this edge to the underside of the arm. Although the tops of staples are exposed here, they are tucked away into the under-side rail of the arm and therefore hidden from view. Then the stapling was completed on the outside back posts and the bottom edge of fabric was taken underneath the chair and stapled to the appropriate rails.

Outside back was stapled with a back-tacking strip along the top. The staples anchoring the sides of this last section cannot be hidden. They were 'topstitched' with staples through back-tacking strips folded into side seam allowances. After the bottom edge was attached to the bottom back rail, any exposed staples were hidden beneath a strip of gimp, glued and pinned into position.

Before covering the front panels, cut through padding on the front faces to the heads of the anchoring nails and pad each one with a coin held in place by a stapled-in Bandaid®. With needle and thread, cobble together the cuts, adding a little more polyester wadding beneath the join if necessary. Cover the panels with fabric, stapling raw edges to panel backs. Muffle hammer head with circles of wadding and fabric secured with thread, position the nails over corresponding holes in arm fronts and drive home the nails with as few strikes as possible so as not to mark the fabric.

HEADBOARDS

PADDED HEADBOARD with REMOVABLE COVER

A headboard which extends beyond the sides of a bed base creates a generous sense of proportion and also presents an opportunity to display a broad 'sweep' of fabric. The queen size bed is 150 cm (5 ft) wide and the headboard is 15 cm (6 in) wider than the bed on both sides; 180 cm (6 ft) wide in total. This silk cover is removable and fastened with bows. To cut costs, its back is a plain, less costly lining fabric which is a similar weight to the silk. Beneath the cover is a calico (muslin) sleeve, padded at the front. This slips over a piece of medium-density fibreboard (MDF) which was cut to the correct size at the store.

Generously proportioned padded headboard with plaid silk cover.

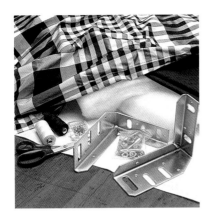

International brackets are bolted to either side of the headboard and fixed to the underside of the bed base by the screws of the castors.

MATERIALS

Fabric for cover, 2.2 m of 150 cm wide (2½ yd of 60 in wide)

Lining fabric for back, 2m of 115 cm wide (2¼ yd of 45 in wide)

Calico (muslin), 6 m of 150 cm wide (6½ yd of 60 in wide)

Medium-density fibreboard (MDF) in a single sheet, 180 cm wide x 110 cm deep (6 ft x 43 in)

Polyester wadding, 2 m of 150 cm wide (2¼ yd of 60 in wide)

Self-adhesive Velcro®, 2.5 m (2¾ yd)

Pins

Scissors

Tape measure

Matching sewing thread

Tailor's chalk

Drill

Sandpaper and sanding block

International brackets for connecting headboard to base (from bedding stores)

Brackets attach the headboard to the bed. In this case, the castors were removed, brackets positioned to enclose the outer edges of the bed base and the castors re-screwed through the appropriate slots in the brackets. To clear the lower front section of upholstery so the bolts to the headboard could be fixed securely without 'play', fabric and padding were cut away and hemmed.

With your own bed head, measure and estimate materials to suit the width of your bed then tailor your cover and padding to fit exactly.

CUTTING OUT

From calico, cut three lining pieces 3 cm (1¼ in) larger all round than the medium-density fibreboard. Cut a piece of wadding the same size as the fibreboard. Cover fabric is cut out later.

ASSEMBLING

With sandpaper and a sanding block, sand any rough edges on the medium-density fibreboard to prevent the fabric catching when the cover is being pulled on.

Calico padding Following Diagram 1, measure the space that will be between the outer edges of brackets when they are fixed to the bed base and mark it onto one piece of calico for the front. Subtract 1.5 cm (⅝ in) from sides and top of this rectangle for seam allowances and cut out the marked area. Use this as a guide to cut the marked area from a second piece of calico and the wadding. With right sides together, stitch along the lower edges and around the cut-away area. Turn right side out. Place the wadding between the calico layers and pin in place.

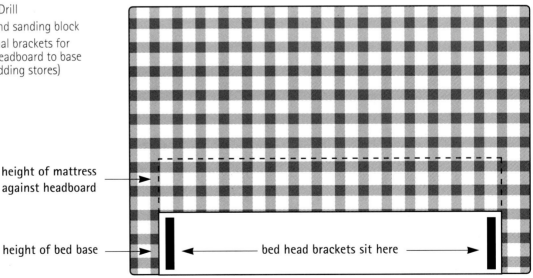

height of mattress against headboard

height of bed base

bed head brackets sit here

Diagram 1

1 Sanding rough edge on the medium-density fibreboard.

2 Mark out the rectangular shape of the bed base on the calico and cut it away.

3 Forming the padding for front headboard. Gap in padding marks the bed base position.

4 Self-adhesive Velcro® holds flaps at the bed base cut-away securely in position.

5 Drilling holes through the headboard to take the bolts for brackets.

Calico sleeve Narrow hem the lower edge of the remaining piece of calico for the back. With right sides together, pin the front and back together along the sides and upper edge. Stitch together and turn right side out. Press the seams. Slip the cover over the fibreboard. Apply self-adhesive Velcro® to hold the flaps formed by the bed base cut-away to the board.

Drill holes Unscrew the castors. Position the brackets where they will be screwed to the bed base, then screw the castors back in place through one of the slots in the brackets. Lifting the calico cover out of the way, hold the headboard against the brackets and mark the position for the holes. Using a drill bit the same size as the bolts, drill the holes. Place the bolt from the back of the headboard to the front so it will not gouge holes in the wall. Unbolt the headboard to make the slip cover.

Making the slip cover front Lay the fabric over the headboard. Take care to centre any design if necessary and allow for a hem at the bottom. Pin it in place and mark the same cut-away shape on the lower edge as for the calico. Allow 3 cm (1¼ in) for hems of the cut-away and cut out the shape. Press 1 cm (³⁄₈ in), then 2 cm (¾ in) to the wrong side and stitch the hem in place.

6 Measuring the shape for the cut-away for the bed base on the headboard cover.

7 Lining in a co-ordinating color has been stitched to the more expensive decorative fabric.

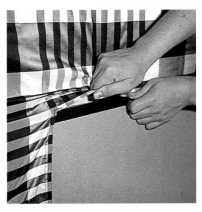

8 Velcro® has been attached around the front cut-away shape of the cover and the front of the fibreboard.

9 Hand stitching fabric ties to the back opening.

10 Cover is fastened at the back with tied bows.

Making the slip cover back Replace the fabric on the bed head and cut it 15 cm (6 in) larger than the sides and top of the headboard. Fold the corners to the back and mitre them. Stitch the corners. Following Diagram 2, cut two backs from co-ordinating plain fabric, adding seam allowances on all sides. Turn under and machine hem a vertical side on each piece for the centre back. With right sides together, stitch the lining to the front. Turn and press the seams. Hem the lower edges of the front and back.

Finishing Slip the cover over the headboard. Other than at the corners, this should fit loosely. Attach Velcro® around the front cut-away shape of the cover and correspondingly on the fibreboard front to hold cover in place. Make fabric ties and hand stitch them in place on both sides of the back opening. Tie the bows to secure the back opening.

decorative fabric

add seam allowance on all sides of the inset panels

inset panel of lining fabric

inset panel of lining fabric

Diagram 2

BUTTONED HEADBOARD
and COVERED BED BASE

Top: Buttoned headboard with new cover and re-styled rounded corners. Inset: Headboard with legs removed prior to being stripped.

The beauty of putting a new cover on a previously buttoned piece of furniture is that you can work from a ready-made pattern – the old cover. Because fabric is dragged down into each depression in the course of buttoning, it has to be somewhat larger than the solid base. You can calculate this by measuring the horizontal and vertical distances between consecutive buttons in the longest and deepest rows and adding 20 cm (8 in) to both these measurements for handling. You can even plot, plan and draw a paper buttoning pattern to transfer to the fabric, starting from the central button and working out along horizontal, vertical and diagonal lines. But doing it this way, especially for the first time, makes the whole process self-explanatory and prepares you admirably for buttoning from scratch in the future.

This headboard was bought inexpensively at a sale. Because I felt its upper corners were a bit sharp I decided to round them off and accentuate the border by covering it in a different fabric. The border fabric was also

MATERIALS

Marking pencil
Pencil
Jig saw
Plain fabric for bed head
Co-ordinating stripe
fabric for border and
sides of bed base
Co-ordinating plain
fabric for piping
Calico (muslin) for
covering buttons and
platform of bed base
Polyester wadding (batting)
Scissors
Staple gun
Cardboard back-
tacking strips
Spray adhesive
Curved needle
Linen thread

used on the bed base, but only on its vertical planes with extra wide calico (muslin) on the platform's top. The slightly concave sides of the bed base were padded out with two thicknesses of polyester wadding (batting).

Although the headboard's central section is broader than most fabrics I was able to run plain fabric along it lengthwise with the selvedge parallel to the top and bottom (called railroading) and therefore, avoid a join.

The diamond-shaped pattern defined by pleats between two offset buttons is dependent on the fabric being cut on the straight grain. Always work with fabric that is accurately squared off and align the centres of the top and bottom and sides of the cover with the corresponding marks on the buttoned section of the headboard.

HEADBOARD

Starting with the lining on the back, strip cover by prising away staples with a screwdriver and pliers. Reserve back lining to be used later, foam surround for the border, both pieces of piping (which turned out to be lengths of plastic tubing) and covers.

1 Use pliers and screwdriver to remove staples.

2 Removing border fabric and piping from headboard.

3 Plate used to form profile of rounded corner.

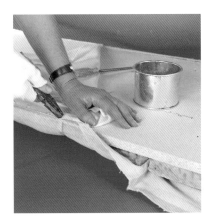

4 When released, fabric from the buttoned section extends beyond the full width of the headboard.

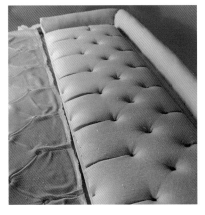

5 Foam molded by the buttoning and edge pleating.

6 Pinning and marking button positions through to right side of new fabric.

7 Cutting out fabric circles and covering buttons.

8 Threading prongs of button through cover fabric.

9 Attaching button prongs to back of headboard.

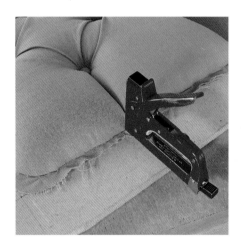

10 Stapling buttoned section to headboard front.

Use a plate to draw the rounded profile before shaping the top corners of particleboard headboard with a jig saw. Remove staples from the edge of central buttoned section of cover and label top and bottom with marking pen. Leave the central piece of foam in place.

Lay old cover over new fabric, and with pins and pencil, mark positions for buttons on the right side of new fabric. Cut away scalloped profile on upper edge of cover following the pattern from the old cover.

To re-cover buttons: a champagne flute proved to be the right size to make patterns for new button covers. With pencil, draw around the lip of an inverted glass and cut out circles of fabric. With needle and thread (knotted at the end), make a row of fine running stitches close to the circle's edge. Place button on stitched circle of fabric, tightly draw up the thread over the button, distribute gathers evenly for a smooth surface and fasten off by stitching back and forth several times through the gathers.

Lay new cover over foam-covered section of headboard, aligning button placement marks on fabric with corresponding holes in foam. Starting at the

11 Cutting bias strips for the piping on both sides of the border.

12 Securing gathers at corners with pins prior to stapling.

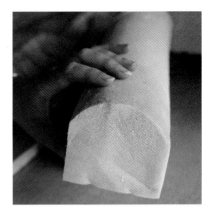

13 End of border foam eventually regained its original 'loaf topped' shape when released from upholstery.

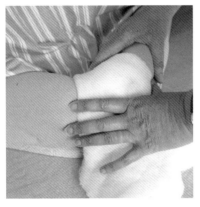

14 Binding the tucked-under corner with wadding.

15 Stapling border foam through border fabric seam allowance.

16 Lining fabric is pinned over facing prior to stapling.

centre of the top row and gripping both prongs of a button together, push them through the fabric and out the hole on the back of the particle board. Separate the prongs and open them out to secure the button temporarily. Push fabric from button to edge into the channel cut in foam. Working in a horizontal line, button each side of the centre, then move down to the next row and start forming the first half of the diamond pattern that is typical of buttoned furniture. Use a regulator or knitting needle to tuck the fabric evenly under both sides of the pleat. Move to the bottom row, completing a diamond, then work out in both directions until all buttons are in place and excess fabric around the edge is tucked into channels.

By jamming one side of the headboard vertically in a bookcase with the rest supported by a table, I was able to work on both the front and back of the headboard, without constantly having to turn it from one side to another.

Once satisfied with the pleating between the buttons, turn the headboard face down and fix the button prongs in place with staples.

Staple edge of the buttoned section of fabric to the headboard front, first shaping the two upper corners of foam with scissors.

Fold piping fabric diagonally and cut and machine join sufficient strips to cover both pieces of the plastic tube. Staple the smaller of the two pieces around the buttoned section, matching raw edges of the piping with the raw edges of the fabric.

Join sufficient fabric for the border and starting from the centre top with the mid point of the fabric, staple it to the headboard front over the piping, raw edges matching. At the corners, use pins to form gathers before stapling.

Starting at the mid point of the lower edge of the border, staple the foam border to the headboard front at 8 cm (3 in) centres. The right angle corners of the border piece of foam had been mitred and glued. Rather than cutting into the corners to round them off, I decided to fold them under and 'bandage' the surface with a strip of wadding, stapled first in the corner and then onto the back.

Fold border fabric over to the back and, starting from the centre, pull it firmly and evenly and staple it to the headboard back.

At lower edge of the headboard, take the fabric hanging from the button-ed section and the borders and pulling it firmly, staple it to the back of the headboard.

Cut a 10 cm (4 in) wide facing from plain fabric for the back. Then staple the piping to the back, starting at the centre of the top, so it makes a neat edge on the outside of the headboard. Over this, back tack the facing match-ing outer raw edge with raw edges of piping, easing the fabric at the corners by cutting into it (the calico lining will cover these slashes) and snipping the inside edge of cardboard back-tacking strip at the corners. Fold facing over to face the right way and pin and 'top stitch' lining fabric to the back with staples.

BED BASE

It is convenient not to have to piece the fabric for the platform of the bed base. Because the bed is king size I bought the widest possible calico. An old bed sheet the right size would do just as well.

Remove mattress, spread calico over the platform and trim it to the size determined by the ridge of the piping. Remove and reserve this piece.

The padding was assembled from two strips of polyester wadding long enough to wrap around the sides and foot with 10 cm (4 in) returns at the head. The first was cut wide enough to be stitched to the piping on the platform's top and stapled to the base's underside. The second was cut just under half this width and glued to the centre line of the wider wadding with spray adhesive. To cope with the bulk of the two layers of wadding after they have been sprayed with adhesive, roll them into a 'bale' and sit on it. Your weight will assist the fixing process.

Measure the depth of the base, add to this at least 20 cm (8 in). This is the width of the decorative fabric for the base. Piece together and stitch sufficient fabric of this width to go around the sides, head and foot of the base adding 15 cm (6 in) for each corner pleat – 60 cm (24 in) in all.

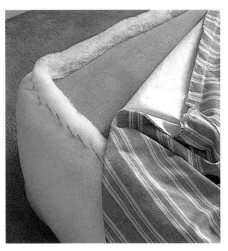

17 Base cover being fitted over the hand-stitched wadding.

18 To accommodate padding, bed base has an inverted pleat at each corner.

When spray adhesive is dry, unfurl the wadding. Find the centre of the wadding's length and match this to the centre point of the foot of the base. With curved needle and linen thread, stitch the edge of the wadding to the piping at the top of the platform. On some bed bases, there is timber beneath the fabric covering the platform and you can fasten the wadding with staples. Lean the base against a wall with the underside facing you. Staple wadding through the fabric of the base to timber rails.

Place base on floor again, right side up, and spread calico on platform top, matching corners. Find centre point of the length of decorative fabric for the vertical planes of the base and match it with the centre of the foot end of the calico. With right sides together, start pinning from the centre to the corners, taking 5 cm (2 in) seam allowance.

At each corner, stop pinning the seam, measure off 15 cm (6 in) and commence pinning again at this point. Fold the resulting flap down on itself to make an inverted pleat, with its mid point over the angle of the corner and equal sides pinned to the seam allowance. Finish pinning to the calico at the centre point of the head then continue pinning down to close the seam of the base fabric.

Remove from platform and sew seams on the machine. Return cover to base, right side up, and smooth fabric to underside.

Lean the base against a wall with the underside facing you and staple fabric to the timber rails on the underside, forming inverted pleats to match those on the platform corners.

THE ART OF DISGUISE

Although loose covers always alter the appearance of seating, this notion can be taken a couple of steps further and a cover used as a veritable cloak of disguise. Black leather furniture is very serious, durable, comfortable and sensible but it has a rather heavy presence that does not always suit the mood of light-hearted decor.

The Corbusier *chaise longue*, for instance, is a great piece designed in 1927 which purists will claim cannot be tampered with. Always willing to test the boundaries of taste and elegance, I devised two different outfits for the *chaise longue*. The raffia-fringed version conjures up the feeling of an island holiday, while the recycled gold curtain fabric and brown silk wrapped legs (see page 99) give this Corb. classic more than a hint of Louis the something.

Above: The Corbusier chaise longue.
Right: Button-ended bolster is held by raffia plaits tied underneath the frame.

MATERIALS

Sufficient fabric

Contrasting fabric for
bolster cover ends

Scraps of lining fabric
for the inner lining of
bolster ends

2 large self-cover buttons

Piping cord

Pins

Scissors

Tape measure

Matching sewing thread

Raffia

Plastic-covered wire
coat hanger

Pliers

Letter clips

7 mm ($^5/_{16}$ in) satin ribbon

48 cm (19 in) zip fastener

Seam tape

Polyester toy filling for
padding bolster cover ends

The basic *chaise longue* has a seat pad which can be unbuckled and removed. Take it off and use it as the pattern for the fabric, drawing around it onto fabric or brown paper. Remember to add seam allowances before cutting out.

I made a separate bolster filled with polyester stuffing with raffia-plaited straps for fastening, preferring to leave the original bolster undisturbed. The bolster's cover is padded a little at both ends so the covered buttons can be anchored to the inner lining through the padding to imitate the traditional buttoned end cap.

The 19 cm (7½ in) raffia fringe hides the distinctive undercarriage of the chaise. Despite investigating every possible avenue of offbeat haberdashery, I was unable to locate raffia fringing, so I had to make my own. With the raffia hat-plaiting craze still in full flight, the raw material was not difficult to find and I constructed a frame from a plastic-covered wire coat hanger around which I wound raffia. I suppose I could have tacked the raffia in place to stabilise it before stitching it onto satin ribbon on the sewing machine, but I used letter clips instead. This system worked quite well although the clips did scratch the free arm and stitch plate of my sewing machine.

Using the seat pad as a pattern for cutting out the cover.

CUTTING OUT

If possible, unbuckle the seat pad and use as a pattern adding 1 cm (³/₈ in) all around. If not, place the fabric on the chaise, right side up. With pins, mark the edge of the seat. Cut out 1 cm (³/₈ in) beyond the pins. Measure the circumference of the bolster and cut a strip of print fabric to this measurement plus 2 cm (³/₄ in) by the width of the bolster (as it sits across the chaise) plus 2 cm (³/₄ in). The plain-colored bolster ends are 10 cm (4 in) by the bolster circumference plus 2 cm (³/₄ in). The fabric for the gathered piping is cut on the bias, two and a half times the bolster's circumference. From scraps of lining, cut two circles of fabric 2 cm (³/₄ in) larger than the finished diameter of the bolster ends. Cut circles for self-cover buttons following package instructions.

ASSEMBLING

Making the Fringe

With pliers, bend the coat hanger into a 'U' shape about 20 cm x 40 cm (8 in x 16 in) with one short side open. Use another piece of wire to make a 'gate' for the open side which is looped around the end of one long side permanently. The other end of the 'gate' should be able to clip on and off the remaining corner.

With the 'gate' closed, wind the raffia around the long sides of the frame. When sufficient thickness has been achieved, use letter clips to stabilise the strands.

1 Winding and clipping raffia to a frame made from a bent coathanger.

2 Machine stitching along one side to anchor the strands of raffia.

3 Cutting the unsewn edge to release fringe from the winding frame.

4 Stitching separate sections of anchored fringe to satin ribbon to make one long piece.

Overleaf: Raffia fringed 'resort wear' for a classic piece of furniture.

When the frame is full, insert zipper foot and place the opening corner edge of the gate just behind the back of the foot and stitch through the strands 1.5 cm (⅝ in) from the right-hand edge of the wound raffia to anchor them, removing the clips as you progress.

To release the stitched raffia, squeeze the two long sides of frame together, insert scissors and cut the raffia free on the side opposite the stitching. Open the 'gate', slide the stitched fringe off the frame and repeat the process.

Continue until you have sufficient fringe to encircle the fabric. Insert ordinary sewing foot and join all the pieces together by stitching them to the length of ribbon over the line of anchoring stitching, jamming the end of one against the beginning of the next to hide joins. Further strengthen the bond between raffia and ribbon with two more rows of machine stitching.

Making the Cover
Machine stitch the wrong side of the fringe to the right side of the cover and place over the chaise.

Making the Gathered Piping
Using a zipper foot, stitch the strip of bias-cut fabric over a long piece of piping cord. Fasten one end of the cord and fabric with a pin and gather up the fabric along the cord until it is the correct length for the circumference of the bolster end, plus seam allowance.

Covering the Bolster
With right sides together, and leaving a gap for the zip fastener, seam both end sections of the long edges of the print fabric. Install the zip fastener, following manufacturer's instructions. Turn right side out.

Stitch two short ends of plain fabric (bolster ends) together, right sides together. Press over 1.5 cm (⅝ in) to the wrong side on one edge of the plain fabric. Stitch to make a casing. Thread seam tape through the casing.

To make bolster end: Firstly align seam of bolster end (plain fabric) with join of gathered piping when formed into a circle and seam line of bolster cover. With a zipper foot, stitch together lining fabric circle, plain fabric bolster end, gathered piping and print fabric with raw edges even and right sides together. Lightly fill bolster end with toy filling before gathering up seam tape and tying in firm knot. Stitch a self-cover button on each end, anchoring it to the inside surface of the lining circle. Insert the bolster into the cover and place the bolster on the *chaise longue*. Make a raffia plait to secure the bolster to the frame and stitch it to the seam of the bolster. Thread the plait through the raffia fringe and tie bolster to the back of the frame.

Curtain fabric, fringe, buttons and bows give a modern classic a hint of a much earlier era.

LOUIS/CORB. CHAISE LONGUE

Fragile, sun-damaged fabric inspired this particular treatment of the *chaise longue*. Originally curtains, they left their first home when a widow of mature years moved from her family residence to a smaller house in a far-away beach resort. For ten or more years after this they received the full force of the sun in their second home which caused them to rot in a most beguiling way that smacked of shabby elegance.

The curtains were unpicked from their heading tape and gently washed to remove dust and grime and the lengths sorted to find pieces suitable for a cover.

To hide the chrome of the *chaise longue*'s undercarriage, a fringed skirt was added to the top which was in turn 'hitched up' with fabric bows.

The bolster is fastened at the back of the *chaise longue* with a shiny twisted cord and the legs are swathed in brown silk which is tied with ochre-colored rattail (a silky, untwisted cord).

MATERIALS

Recycled fabric
Contrasting silk or satin fabric
Pins
Scissors
Tape measure
Matching sewing thread
Fringe
Rattail
Satin cord
8 self-cover buttons
Seam tape

CUTTING OUT

If possible, unbuckle the seat pad and use as a pattern, adding 1 cm (³⁄₈ in) all around. If not, place the fabric on the *chaise longue*, right side up. With pins, mark the edge of the seat. Cut out 1 cm (³⁄₈ in) beyond the pins. Measure around the perimeter of the seat. Add extra fabric to make small pleats at corners and bends where necessary. For the skirt, cut fabric strips 30.5 cm (12 in) wide to fit rather loosely around the edge of the seat, adding 1 cm (³⁄₈ in) for joining seams where necessary. Cut a strip of fabric for the bolster cover, 10 cm (4 in) longer than the bolster and the circumference plus 2 cm (³⁄₄ in). Cut a strip of fabric 20 cm x 2 m (8 in x 2 yards 8 in) for the bows.

ASSEMBLING

Joining seat and skirt Join the skirt pieces to form a loop. With right sides together, pin the skirt to the seat, adding small pleats at corners and bends where necessary. Place the cover on the *chaise longue* and make any necessary adjustments. Stitch together. Hem the lower edge and stitch the fringe over the hem.

Bows are made from fabric squares pinched in the middle with silk covered buttons on top.

Making bows Cut the bow strip into eight pieces each 20 x 25 cm (8 x 10 in). Fold each strip in half crosswise (20 x 12.5 cm). Stitch together around three sides, leaving a small opening for turning in one side. Turn right side out, press and stitch the opening closed. With needle and double thread, make small running stitches along centre of bow and gather. Secure the thread. Cover the buttons with the silk fabric, following the manufacturer's instructions. Stitch the buttons to the centres of each bow.

Attaching bows Place the cover on the *chaise longue*. Decide on the bow positions. Corners and bends tend to be the usual choices. Hand pleat the fabric at these positions and tack the pleats in place. Then tack a bow over each of these positions.

Adding ties Decide on the best position for ties. This is usually at each end, and at any bends along the sides, or at two evenly spaced intervals along the side. From seam tape, cut ties long enough to be tied beneath the *chaise longue*. Remove the cover and stitch the ties in place in the seam allowances.

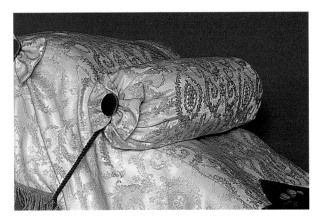

Satin cord holds the bolster fast.

Covering feet Lay a large piece of fabric under one foot. Gather the fabric up around the foot and tie it in place with rattail. Secure the ends. Gather the remaining fabric at the top of the leg and secure with seam tape. Trim any excess fabric. Repeat for the remaining legs.

Covering the bolster With right sides facing, sew the long edges together with a 1 cm ($^3/_8$ in) seam. Turn right side out. Press 1.5 cm ($^5/_8$ in) to the wrong side on both ends. Stitch to make a casing, leaving a small opening. Thread seam tape through the casing. Place the bolster in the cover. Thread the cord through the cover with an equal amount hanging at each end. Pull the tape to gather and secure. Stitch a bow on each end. Place the bolster on the *chaise longue*. Pass the cord around to the back of the *chaise longue* and tie it in place.

SOFT-LOOK SOFA

The peach-colored Indian cotton used here to convert a rather leaden black leather sofa into a sumptuous seat had already endured an earlier life as curtains. Although there was a serious overdose of peach in the eighties, it was a pleasure to work with this color again because it is very soothing to the eyes.

Above: Two-seater black leather sofa.
Right: A snipped and stitched seam gives shaping and depth to this upper back corner of the cover.
Overleaf: Sofa is resplendent in an 'ice-cream cake' cover with a hobbled padded skirt.

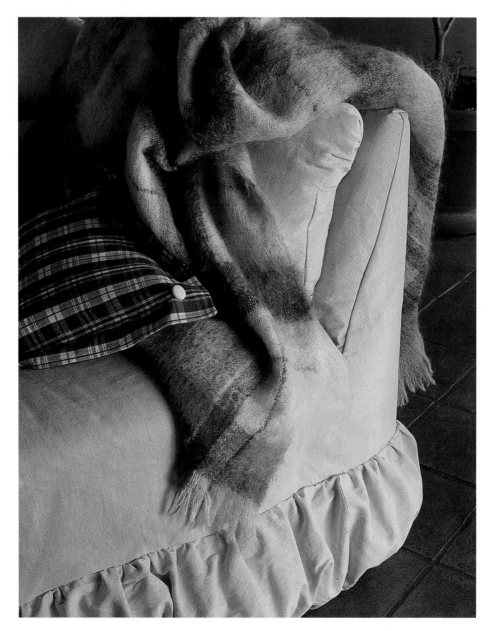

MATERIALS

Sufficient fabric
Scissors
Pins
Tape measure
Fabric marker
Matching sewing thread
Polyester wadding
Standard curtain
gathering tape

A 'hobbled' skirt, padded with polyester wadding, puddles on the floor like pastel-colored whipped cream. Because of the heavy weight of fabric, standard gathering curtain tape was used to ruffle the skirt. A random assortment of bright cushions further enhances the relaxed mood.

This cover has been made to fit loosely and slips on to the sofa without need for fastenings. If this will not work for your sofa, leave an opening at one or both corner back seams and stitch Velcro® to both sides, or have placket openings down both rear corners with ties on both sides.

CUTTING OUT

Remove the cushions from the sofa. Back cushions were held fast with zippers (one side of zipper on the inside back, the other on the cushion's back) and seat cushions were fastened with straps and buckles to a lower back rail down the seat crevice.

Cut a piece 2.5 cm (1 in) smaller all around than the seat platform. Pin it in place and, measuring from here, measure and cut the following, adding 2.5 cm (1 in) for ease and seams to all edges, and 20 cm (8 in) to lower edges for hems. Cut an inside back, an outside back and front gusset (section at front between floor and seat cushions). Cut the arms in one piece from the floor going over the top of the arm to the seat platform. In this case there was sufficient fabric to include the arm front, extending it at right angles. Plan for the seam joining the outside back and inside back to fall at the back of the sofa, and for the seam between the front gusset and seat platform to be covered by the cushions.

Cut cushion covers noting any unusual shaping; the back cushions have a scoop at their lower outside corners. Back cushion covers were cut with a slit to accommodate their zipper fastenings. Slots were left in the underside of seat cushions for strap attachments.

Cut a 35 cm (14 in) deep ruffle strip measuring twice the circumference of the sofa.

ASSEMBLING
Slipcover
When sewing, stitch closer than usual to the fabric's raw edge so the resulting seam is narrower than usual – which gives the cover a relaxed, loose fit.

Pin the cover on the sofa with the wrong side facing you and mark the seam lines with a fabric marker. Remove the cover and stitch the pieces together, one at a time, in the following order: stitch the outside back to the inside back, then the front gusset to the seat platform. Stitch the arms to the inside back and outside back, then to the seat.

This sofa has rounded corners which can be accounted for without too much intricate tucking and pleating. With right sides together, flatten out a stitched pointed corner, seamline in the centre and seam allowance pressed flat, and stitch across the corner. Cut away the triangular scrap of waste fabric and turn to right side; the corner now has depth. (See detail picture on page 101.)

Arms
Prior to stitching the front corner and front gusset seams of the arm fronts, mark and stitch darts or pleats in the arms so that the cover loosely fits the shape of the arms.

Gathered Skirt
Hem the lower edge of the slipcover. With right sides together, join the short ends of the ruffle strip to form a loop. Stitch gathering tape to the right side of the strip along the two long edges. Gather the upper edge of the ruffle to fit around the sofa and pin the ruffle in place. Remove the slipcover. With right sides together, stitch the ruffle to the slipcover at the edge of the gathering tape, taking care not to catch the tape in the stitching. Replace the slipcover on the sofa. Gather the lower tape tightly to fit under the sofa. If desired, add a small amount of wadding behind the ruffle to pad it out.

Back and Seat Cushions
When stitching cushion covers, refer to existing cushions and note that these covers are more closely fitted than the slipcover.

TWO-SEATER SOFA

MATERIALS

Screwdriver

Needle-nosed pliers

Hammer

Steel wool

Solution of half gum turpentine and half methylated spirits

Beeswax furniture polish

Fabric marker

Scissors

Pins

Staple gun

Tack hammer

Tacks

Cardboard back-tacking strips

Curved needle

Twine

Calico (muslin)

Hessian (burlap)

12 mm (½ in) foam for seat, inside back and inside arms

30 mm (1¼ in) foam for cushions

Polyester wadding (batting)

Linters

Sufficient upholstery fabric

Spray adhesive

Flexible metal tacking strip

Gimp

White glue (PVA for wood)

2 zippers for seat cushions

Top: Sofa in its original state, cushions removed.

Right: The finished sofa.

Six fabrics featuring dots, stars, flowers, foliage and exotic African animals were combined to give a decrepit two-seater a glorious coat of many colors. Originally from the USA, the sofa seemed at first glance to be in a fairly advanced state of decay. Stuffing at the front of the seat had descended to the spring cavity through a large tear in the hessian. The two foam-filled loose cushions which had probably been added to compensate for the dip in the seat, were perished. As this project was to be an exercise in colorful upholstery, the cushions were retained (new ones were made) and used to display additional pattern and color.

Because repairing the seat seemed to be such an enormous task, I decided to give it some thought while starting on the inside back.

STRIPPING

I left the springing of the seat intact, hoping that it might be salvageable. Although the hessian on top of the springs had given way, the webbing, spring lashings and the stitching of the springs to the hessian were sound.

The stripping started at the outside back and as the layers came off, foam which had perished with age was discarded. However the coir fibre packing from the outside back edge of the seat and the cotton padding were reserved. Piping and front edge roll of the seat were saved and the old covers retained to be used as patterns.

With the outside back exposed, arched zigzag springs with their coil spring links were revealed between upper and lower back rails.

The removal of staples and tacks resulted in a considerable heap of scrap metal. The stripping stage is dull compared to the fun of dealing with fabrics and trims later on and this process invariably takes much longer than anticipated.

Re-finishing the Woodwork

The varnish on the front and back legs and the grooved exposed part of the lower frame was brittle and came off easily with a scraper. The turps/methylated spirits solution was rubbed in with steel wool to clean and smooth the surface. Then the beeswax furniture polish was applied and buffed to a shine.

1 Perished foam cushions, gauze wrapped to prevent further disintegration, became swollen when covers were removed.

2 Ripped hessian covering accounting for dipped seat was revealed when sofa was stripped down to the foam overlay.

3 A former cover was revealed when the seat padding was removed. Front edge roll (on floor) was reserved.

4 Rear view shows zigzag springs between upper and lower rails of the back with cross–connecting coil springs.

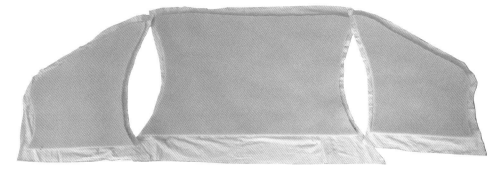

5 Foam and calico undercover was made for the inside back and inside arms.

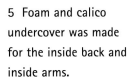

Inside Back and Inside Arms

The original inside back cover was made from four pieces with central piping. The new back is worked in three pieces so the giraffe motif is undisturbed. Cotton wadding in good condition was re-used but new 12 mm (½ in) foam cut in the exact shapes of the inside arms and inside back was secured with spray adhesive to calico pieces (undercovers) cut larger than the foam to give seam allowances.

Prise away staples to release webbing where necessary on underside of frame to gain access to the underside of the lower backrest rail. Finding the centres of fabric and frame (foam to the inside and fabric facing out)

6 Stapling inside back to lower back rest rail. Webbing released from underside of seat rail to gain access.

7 Inside back, joined with piping to inside arms, is stapled in place.

8 Re-stapling the webbing using pliers to tension each strip.

position the inside back undercover first of all and fix with staples to the lower backrest rail, starting at the centre and working out. Attach lower edges of inside arms in the same way.

Attach top edges of calico to top rail of frame with staples, starting at the centre and working out, pulling the calico taut as you go.

Seam together the inside back upholstery fabric with piping between inside arms and inside back. Note slashes on original cover so fabric could be drawn around the posts (upright members) of the frame and transfer to new fabric with marker. Cover calico with a layer of polyester wadding cut to fit the curves of the inside back.

Position piped cover, aligning centre points on frame, and staple in same sequence as foam-and-calico pieces, pulling fabric taut as you go and slashing fabric where necessary to go around joins in the frame. Complete lower edge first and then start from the centre of the top and work out, catching polyester wadding underneath the upholstery fabric. Re-staple webbing in place using pliers and fingers to pull webbing as tight as possible. An extra pair of hands is helpful during this process.

Border

Cut and seam fabric for the border between the inside back/arms and the outside back/arms and cut polyester wadding in the same shape; no need to seam the wadding. Make a piping strip to fit this long join and staple it (starting from the centre point) to the proposed join line of inside back/ arms and border, raw edges matching. Place border fabric with its wadding on wrong side over the piping, right sides together and raw edges matching. Over this, place cardboard back-tacking strip and staple through all layers to frame with edge of strip pressed firmly against the piping cord. Snip other edge of back-tacking strip where necessary to negotiate curves. Pad the timber of the frame with a strip of 12 mm (½ in) foam fixed to the timber with spray adhesive. Fold border fabric over to its right side and staple its edge to the rear of the sofa's upper rail.

Overleaf and inset: Upholstery 'patchwork' of six fabrics using the various planes of the sofa to define the different pieces.

9 Back tacking the border in place. Cardboard strip against piping makes a neat firm edge.

10 Border padded with foam before fabric and wadding strip is stapled to the outside back.

The Seat

To repair the hessian section of the seat, cobble together the tear using a needle and threads pulled from a new piece of hessian. The join is less likely to rip apart when mending threads are compatible with the damaged fabric. Then staple a new piece of hessian over the old following the line of the original. With twine and curved needle, stitch springs to hessian. Working from the centre, replace hessian-covered ready-made edge roll along front of seat, stapling into its flange.

Because I miscalculated the amount of fabric required for the seat, I had to sew calico extension flaps to the rear edge of cover.

Using 12 mm (½ in) foam, spray adhesive, calico and cover fabric, assemble the two-part upholstery for the seat, referring to the original cover. Glue a double thickness of foam to the rear section of the calico undercover, behind the line where the arms meet the seat. It is along this line that the cover fabric is topstitched to the calico (foam should be positioned to clear this line) before the whole assembly is attached to the hessian spring cover using a curved needle and twine. This makes the indentation between front and back of seat.

Top up the original padding at the front of the seat with a layer of linters, pull the undercover to the front and, starting at the centre, staple it to the front rail of frame. At each corner, make an inverted pleat and trim away the excess. Following sequence for undercover, staple cover fabric in place to the edge of the exposed polished timber of front and sides.

Behind the stitching line, pad the hessian with two layers of linters. Push undercover through back and side seat crevices and turn sofa over. Re-using coir fibre, make a firm outside edge, enclose edge with undercover and staple in place at back of frame.

Then push cover fabric through seat crevice and staple to appropriate rails, slashing fabric where necessary to fit around uprights and joins.

11 Stitching through new hessian to anchor springs with curved needle and twine. Catch the top of spring in three or four places.

12 When all the springs are attached to the hessian, edge roll is stapled in place along seat front to the corner and then to the arms.

13 Stitching along the underside of the seat upholstery assembly to make the dividing line between the front and back portions of the seat.

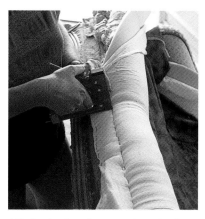

14 New layer of linters added to front seat padding.

15 Beginning from centre, staple front seat padding to the frame.

16 Making an inverted pleat at the corner.

17 Trim away excess foam at corner before stapling cover fabric to edge of frame. Gimp, glued in place, will eventually cover staples.

18 Rear section of seat cover fabric with extension flap is pushed through crevice to back. Slash in fabric will 'straddle' frame joins.

19 Starting at the centre of the rear back rail of frame and working out in both directions, extension flap is stapled in place.

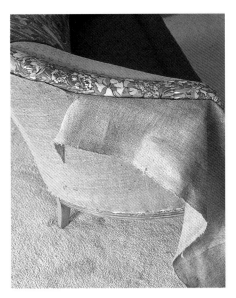

20 Trimming away the hessian lining on the outside back and outside arm.

Outside Back

Cover the whole outside back with hessian in one piece, selvedge parallel to top and bottom (railroaded). Begin stapling straight onto hessian at the centre back, top and bottom, and work out, pulling taut as you go. Trim edges after stapling.

Carefully shielding floor and new cover, spray hessian with adhesive and then roll on a layer of linters. Trim to shape with scissors, sloping padding towards the edges of the frame. Cover linters with a layer of calico, draped, fastened and trimmed in the same way as the hessian.

Cut and stitch outside back in three pieces like the inside back but without piping at seams.

Staple piping to the join line of the outside back and border. Position outside back cover over piping at centre top, right sides together and raw edges matching. Over this, place cardboard back-tacking strip long enough to reach the curves of the arms. Staple through all layers to frame with edge of strip pressed firmly against the piping cord.

Cut off sufficient metal tacking strip for the curve of the arms. Using staple gun and tacks where staples cannot connect with timber, attach the strip so its open edge butts up against piping. Turn down the outside back cover and poke its outside arm edges into the jaws of the tacking strip. Trim away excess fabric. Press jaws closed with fingers. Then close securely with tack hammer until fabric is flattened and stretched taut, softening blows with small cardboard strip.

Pull lower edge of outside back taut and staple to underside of lower rails, starting at the centre and working out.

Trim lower edge of seat front and outside arms up to staples and cover staples with gimp fastened with white glue and held to dry with pins.

To determine the profile of separate cushions accurately, tuck calico into the seat section and, standing behind the sofa with a marker pen held at right angles to the seat and pressed tightly against the back, trace the shape of the back, arms and front of arms onto the calico. Use the shape as a guide when cutting the foam.

These cushions were made with a core of 30 mm (1¼ in) foam covered with two layers of polyester wadding on the top, one on the bottom and with an edging of wadding cobbled to the front and outer edges only.

The undercovers were made of calico.

For the cushion covers, strips for the boxed sides of the cushions in contact with the inside back and inside arms were fitted with zippers. Piping was stitched to all the boxed side strips and then pinned and basted to the tops and bottoms. The tops and bottoms were cut from the pattern for the foam shapes. By combining foam and wadding, the cushions were designed to be soft and comfortable and also to hold their shape.

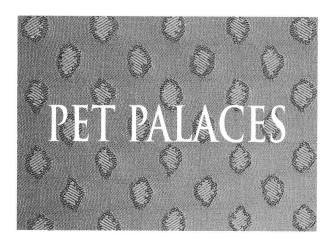

PET PALACES

SUMMER PALACE

What size should a pet palace be? The dimensions of this structure are based on the size of a curled-up cat rather than a stretched-out one. This frame is made of timber and its floor plan measures 47 cm (18½ in) square, externally. It is 81 cm (32 in) high overall, measures 50 cm (19½ in) from roof/frame join to the bottom of lower frame and has 4 cm (1½ in) legs which are extensions of the uprights with 2 cm (¾ in)

MATERIALS

Polyester wadding (batting)

Spray adhesive

2.5 m (2¾ yd) of 137 cm (54 in) wide cover fabric

Scissors

Cardboard back-tacking strips

Staple gun

Strong thread (linen or 4 strands of embroidery floss)

3 m (3½ yd) gimp

Hot glue gun

70 cm (¾ yd) sheer fabric for curtains, 120 cm (48 in) wide

1 m (1 yd) narrow satin ribbon

Ruffle foot for sewing machine

45 cm (18 in) square of fusible wadding (batting)

43 cm (17 in) square of 30 mm (1¼ in) foam

Gauze fabric for wrapping foam

1 m (1 yd) of fabric for cushion and finial

180 cm (2 yd) contrasting piping

57 cm (22 in) zipper

Floral cotton is stretched, bunched and padded to make a pampered pet's summer palace.

A trial run of the timber
frame of the palace
before upholstery.

dowels driven into their undersides as 'feet'. The roof is fairly steeply pitched and rises 24 cm (9½ in) vertically above the roof/frame join. The base is a piece of plywood drilled with ventilation holes. The roof is plywood also and finished with a spherical wooden finial attached to a dowelling peg which is pushed into a hole at the top. Cushion measures 43 cm (17 in) square in 30 mm (1¼ in) foam.

A timber frame gives a sturdy foundation for attaching coverings but I have seen quite satisfactory pet dwellings made from very substantial cardboard cartons. Although fabrics may have to be fastened to cardboard with hot glue instead of staples, spectacular results can be achieved.

Start by cutting four triangles of polyester wadding slightly smaller than roof segments and attaching them to the roof with spray adhesive.

Attaching the Fabric

The structure is first wrapped in fabric like a tube, with one selvedge 1.5 cm (⅝ in) below the bottom of frame. Start by back tacking at one side of the front, taking fabric around the back to the other side front and then across the entrance to the starting point. Allow another 1.5 cm (⅝ in) before snipping and tearing the excess fabric away. Cut away the gap for the entrance leaving 1.5 cm (⅝ in) turn-up on top and side of entrance.

Using cardboard back-tacking strips to make a neat edge but 'top stitching' with the staple gun, attach the fabric to the three bottom edges of the structure, starting at the edge at right angles to the first back-tacked side and pulling firmly on fabric to ensure that each stretched panel is wrinkle free. Use this same method to attach the fabric to the other side front. The top of the entrance can be properly back tacked; mitre the inside corner seam allowance first. Then staple into the line of the roof join at top of sides and back.

Gather loose fabric at the roof top by hand, to decide if 'collar' needs to be shallower than the full fabric width; tear away excess fabric if necessary.

With a needle and strong thread, baste close to the upper edge of fabric. Gather roof top fabric by hand at proposed base of 'collar' and arrange gathers evenly. Then wrap tightly and secure with string, ensuring that join at side front is neatly hidden from view. Pull in the basting thread to gather top of 'collar' and tie off. Starting at the centre back of the lower edge, glue gimp over all the stapled edges, mitring corners.

Curtains

Cut ribbon into three equal pieces and staple each length through the centre to each side and to centre top of entrance.

Machine hem one cut edge of sheer fabric. Gather opposite edge by machine to measure 48 cm (19 in). Back tack curtain top to the inside of the top of the entrance. Gather centre of curtain from the bottom to the top with fingers; secure these gathers with a bow tied in the ribbon. Arrange the swathed gathers at the sides and secure with ribbon bows.

Padded Pelmet

Join together sufficient 20 cm wide strips to make a piece 3.6 m (4 yd) long. Fold in half lengthwise, wrong sides together, over a 6 cm (2½ in) wide strip of wadding, and machine stitch 1.5 cm (⅝ in) from the raw edges. Gather the stitched edge by hand using strong thread and needle or use the machine's ruffling foot. Find centre point of pelmet strip and align it with the centre of entrance top. Starting at this point, back tack with cardboard strips to the roof-line join with raw edges hanging down. Before stapling at the centre back, trim ends, leaving a generous overlap, and fold one end inside the other. Draw padded pelmet down over the back-tacking strip.

Wrapping foam in gauze ensures that the insert will glide easily into the cushion cover.

Cushion

Allowing 1.5 cm (⅝ in) seam allowances on every edge to be sewn, cut two cushion tops, one cushion bottom, one piece for the boxed front and sides (up to the overlap of the zipper). Then cut another shorter boxed section in two equal pieces (lengthwise) to accommodate the zipper.

Following manufacturer's instructions, fuse wadding to one cushion top. Place the second top (right side up) over the wadding, pin together and top stitch with matching thread 10 cm (4 in) from raw edges.

Assemble shorter boxed piece with zipper centred and stitch, right sides together, to short ends of the other boxed piece to make a loop.

Starting at the centre back of cushion top, stitch on piping placing raw edges together and clipping at corners for easing.

With right sides together, pin boxed section loop to cushion top and bottom, marking corners on both edges of boxed piece and clipping nearly to stitching. Stitch in place with zipper foot. Turn right side out. Wrap foam with gauze and insert.

Swathed Finial

From cushion fabric, cut a circle of fabric to cover wooden ball, smooth it over the ball and secure fabric edge around the peg by winding and then knotting string. Alternatively, a tennis ball could be a substitute; hand stitch tied fabric edge to the upper folds of the 'collar'.

WINTER PALACE

Owner in residence in the
winter palace.

The selected fabric pattern with its leaf motif within a banded stripe determined the way the roof and outer covering were cut and pieced together. Fabric matched in weight to the cover was used as a facing to enclose the cotton fringe of the pelmet, skirt, curtain edges and the lower band of sides and back. This facing fabric also forms the platform top.

The golden cupola is one half of a wooden egg. A few stitches in the rooftop upholstery through holes drilled around the edge of the half egg hold it in place.

Finding tassels small enough to trim between the scallops of the skirt and pelmet was difficult. My solution was to buy a piece of fringe which was strung with tiny tassels and snip them free. Then the piece of fringe, minus tassels and bound with twisted cord made from stranded embroidery floss, was arranged around the base of the golden egg cupola.

The tufted cushion cover is made from slinky underwear satin and the 'shirred' interior is just an inexpensive acetate lining, gathered by machine.

Two pieces of foam were used; one for the tufted cushion, the other to raise the level of the platform beneath the cushion to a suitable height for the scalloped skirt.

The beauty of an upholstery project such as this is that it is small, manageable, good fun and gives plenty of scope for opulent treatments and trims.

CUTTING OUT

Cutting and accurate placement ensure successful pattern matching. Measure carefully and transfer all measurements to the fabric before cutting. Make a paper pattern first if there is still any uncertainty.

In this case, the centre stripe of the leaf motif was aligned with the centre top and bottom of each of the four roof segments.

Bands of fabric, plain at the top and cut mid way along the leaf stripe, were scalloped to form the pelmet and skirt. Draw up a paper pattern of the edge using a cup to determine the profile of the scallop and spacing the scallops to ensure the corners of the frame fall between two of them. The pelmet has five scallops between two corners. Cut the pelmet piece long enough for it to be sewn into a loop that fits snugly around the frame.

The outer covering, which has a finished roof-join-to-hemline length of 51 cm (20 in) (plus fringe) is cut in six separate pieces before being sewn together into one assembly. Sides and back are three squares of fabric cut to pattern match the roof fabric. Tied-back curtains with curved lower front corners are cut from an entire leaf stripe with a little of the plain stripe attached for joining at the side seams. The edging band of the sides and back needed more plain stripe on top of the half-leaf stripe to bring the assembly out to its full size.

Cut facings identical to the curtains and edging band.

MATERIALS

Polyester wadding (batting)

Spray adhesive

1.5 m (1¾ yd) of 152 cm (60 in) wide cover fabric

1 m (1 yd) of 120 cm (48 in) facing fabric

1.5 m (1⅔ yd) 90 cm (36 in) wide acetate lining fabric

Ruffle foot for sewing machine

Scissors

Cardboard back-tacking strips

Staple gun

Tacks

Tack hammer

4 m (4½ yd) flat gold trim for pelmet top, curtain and roof

5.25 m (5¾ yd) cotton fringe

1 m (1 yd) silky tasselled fringe

Stranded embroidery thread; 3 gold, 2 maroon, 1 green

Small piece of firm cardboard

Carving fork

3.5 m (4 yd) flanged gold piping for cushion

Hot glue gun

Two 43 cm (17 in) squares of 30 mm (1¼ in) foam

Gauze fabric for wrapping foam

60 cm (⅔ yd) of underwear satin

3 white ostrich feathers

Tea leaves

Hair drier

Half sphere with 9 cm (3½ in) diameter painted gold for cupola

Power drill

Rubber band

Long needle

Two beads

1 Back-tacked roof join showing cardboard strip and roof segment padded with polyester wadding.

2 Last join on roof is slip tacked over a cardboard strip and pinned before being hand stitched closed.

Roof

Cut four triangles of polyester wadding slightly smaller than the segments of the roof and attach to the roof with spray adhesive.

Align centre lines on fabric and front roof segment before stapling in place at the top and bottom and then both sides. Ensure staples are plotted beyond the join lines of neighbouring cover pieces so they will eventually be hidden.

Match pattern carefully for the next roof piece. Slip tack (temporary tack) at top and bottom and check the junction at the sides prior to back tacking permanently with cardboard strip – right sides together and raw edges matching. Draw fabric over to right side, pulling to eliminate wrinkles, and staple at centres of other two sides of the triangle and continue stapling, moving out to the corners in both directions.

Continue this way until ready to close last join. Wrap last free side of roof fabric around cardboard back-tacking strip and slip tack at centre, top and bottom. With needle and thread, slip stitch to close the join. Remove slip tacks.

Attach flat gold trim to the join lines of roof with hot glue gun.

Shirred Lining

Fold acetate lining in two lengthwise, snip and tear to make two pieces each 46 cm (18 in) wide. Seam together to make a single piece 3 m (3¼ yd) long and gather each long side to measure 1.35 m (1½ yd) using ruffle foot on sewing machine. Making sure right side of lining will face the interior of the palace and with centre join of lining aligned with centre top of inside back, back tack with cardboard strip to back and sides of ceiling, turning under a hem's depth at the front.

Draw fabric down to right side and staple to inside lower edge of frame. The staples will show but will eventually be covered by the cushion.

Outer Covering

After cutting fabric to make the outer covering, stitch the pieces together starting with the back and sides. Then add the edging band and top stitch flat gold trim over seam line. Finally add the two curtain pieces.

Join back and side facing to lower outside edges of curtain facing.

Cut off sufficient fringe in one piece to go down the two sides and around bottom of the outer covering. Place fringe heading on edge of right side of fabric with fringe end towards centre of outer covering. Position facing over fringe, right sides together with heading and outside raw edges matching. Pin and sew seam. Trim away the heading of cotton fringe if bulky. Secure fringe with another row of stitching before trimming. Turn and press.

Align centre back of top of outer covering with centre back of roof-line join, matching fabric pattern and with cardboard back-tacking strip, back tack towards front. At front, make three even pleats for curtain top before back tacking.

Pelmet

Cut and pin individual lengths of cotton fringe for curves; bulky heading of fringe makes it impossible to negotiate the points between two curves. Fringe is sandwiched between the right sides of the facing and pelmet fabric with the fringe heading and cut edges of the curves matching, and fringe ends pointing to the centre. Pin and machine sew curved edges. Sew a second row of stitching over the first before trimming away bulky heading. Turn and press.

With right sides together and raw edges matching, sew the short sides of pelmet together to make a loop. Press seam flat.

Turn under raw edges of pelmet fabric and facing on the remaining open long side and top stitch closed, close to the edge.

Top stitch flat gold trim to upper edge of pelmet, joining ends at short seam of pelmet.

Platform and Skirt

Wrap one piece of foam in gauze. Make a piece of scalloped edging (the skirt) to fit the front of the platform (five scallops across) following the directions for the pelmet but sewing down the short sides when stitching the fringe between facing and front.

Cut a piece of facing to cover the platform 2 cm (¾ in) wider than the skirt and about 63 cm (25 in) long. With right sides together, seam a centred short side of platform cover to the skirt front. Press seam toward fringe edge, fold in the hem of the skirt facing and top stitch closed. Turn under scant hems on other three sides of platform cover and sew.

Tuck the platform cover around the rear of foam, adjusting to find correct length for hem.

Tufted Cushion

Cut a square of polyester wadding the same size as the cushion top. Cut and stitch a box-sided cushion cover from underwear satin with flanged

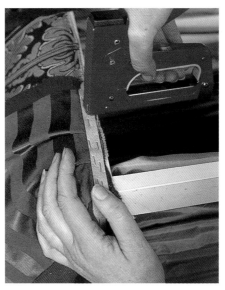

3 Top of curtain is back tacked to the top of entrance.

4 Using a cup to gauge the profile of the scalloped pelmet and skirt.

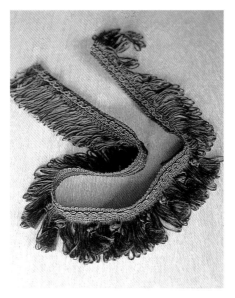

5 Length of silky fringe with some tassels removed to trim pelmet and skirt.

6 Platform cover is joined to skirt. Shirred interior is acetate lining fabric.

gold piping at the top and bottom edges. This cover is not removable; leave one side open, insert foam, arrange wadding square on top and pin and hand stitch the opening closed.

Make 13 tufts with embroidery floss wound around a rigid form with a gap in the middle. Upholsterers use a winding stick made from hardwood with smooth edges and a groove cut down the middle. I use a stainless steel carving fork. Enclose each one with an embroidery floss slip knot (see page 65) leaving plenty of trailing thread before sliding tuft off. Pull slip knot tight. Starting 9 cm (3½ in) from outside edges, plot nine equally spaced tufting positions (three rows of three) on cushion top. From facing fabric, cut nine small squares of fabric. Thread tails of slip knot through large needle, and stitch through a

Opposite: Pet palace in all its finery trimmed with feathers and fringes.

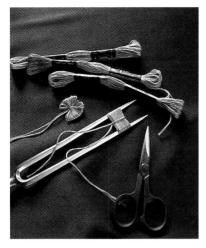

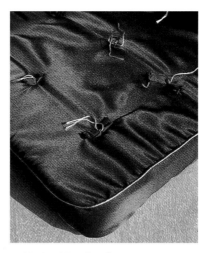

8 Using carving fork as a winding stick for making tufts.

9 Underside of tufted cushion with threads knotted over scraps of facing fabric.

10 Front face of wadding topped cushion is pulled into deep depressions by tufts.

11 Feathers go into the cupola top. Glued twisted cords hold fringe and form a 'collar'.

12 On each pelmet corner, a trio of tassels on a common floss-wound 'stalk' is topped by a tuft with a maroon centre.

13 Curtain tie-back is a tri-coloured twisted cord ending in a homemade tassel with five tiny tassels tied to its waist.

tufting position to the underside of cushion. Take thread ends out of needle and tie another slip knot around a rolled-up square of facing fabric.

When all nine tufts are in place, tighten slip knots, ensuring that tufts are evenly pulled down on the top of cushion and fasten off with a half hitch (see page 65).

Feather-topped Cupola

Dye white feathers by boiling them in water and tea leaves for ten minutes. Rinse under cold water, pat dry between paper towels and dry with a hair drier. When wet, they look beyond redemption but they quickly fluff up again when blasted with hot air.

Drill holes through wooden rim of half sphere and drill a hole in its top large enough to accept the quills of the three feathers. Position half sphere on point of roof and with long needle and thread, stitch through rim holes into cover fabric. Fasten off.

With scissors, release tiny tassels from silky fringe and reserve for the tasselled trims – I needed 42 in all. The fringe looked a bit thin at this stage so I used two layers around the rim of the half sphere. The first was glued (using a hot glue gun) with the wrong side of the heading against the rim with a lapped-over join at the back. For the second, I turned the fringe upside down and glued the wrong side of its heading over the right side of the first heading. The cascading 'tendrils' of the second application were held in check by two rows of twisted cord made from gold stranded embroidery floss and fastened with hot glue. To make a twisted cord, just restrain one end of a length of floss, twist the other end in one direction pulling it tight, divide in two along its length with your other hand and allow both half-lengths to twist around one another equally. Smooth out any tangles then knot the cut ends together.

Bind quills with a rubber band and poke into hole in top of half sphere.

TASSELLED TRIMS

Curtain tassels Make two thicker twisted cords at least 45 cm (18 in) long with all three colors of stranded embroidery floss for curtain tie-backs and knot a bead at one end of each. Wind half of a skein of embroidery thread around a 13 cm (5 in) square piece of firm cardboard, cut to release threads at both ends and arrange threads evenly around the bead and tie a single strand very tightly above it with two thirds of the length of the threads above the bead. Draw the longer threads down over the bead and secure with more wound thread to made a waisted tassel. Wind some more contrasting thread over the junction between cord and bead and finish by stitching thread end into tassel. Trim bottom off evenly. Attach five of the tiny tassels snipped from the fringe to the larger tassel's waist. Release stitching at an appropriate part of the curtain side seam and hand stitch a loop of twisted cord to the facing side of curtain seam. Thread the other end with the tassel behind the shirred lining, then around the curtain edge and through the loop.

Pelmet corner tassels With a needle threaded with embroidery floss, stitch from the underside of a pelmet corner to the right side, then through the looped top of a snipped tassel and back into the pelmet to the underside (in the same place) leaving the tassel dangling by 2 cm (3/4 in). Repeat for two more tassels. Bring needle through again to the right side and bind the tassels together by winding floss to make a common 'stalk'. Repeat for three remaining pelmet corners.

Wind the centres of the four remaining gold tufts with a contrasting color of embroidery floss and stitch over the tops of tassel stalks.

Sew a snipped tassel between scallops of skirt and pelmet. Slip pelmet loop over roof and arrange with tasselled tufts at corners.

CHILDREN'S CHAIRS

The two cane children's chairs covered here seemed, at first glance, to be similar. But one has a circular seat and the other has its seat border, seat and inside back woven in one undulating piece. These shapes suggested entirely different configurations for their respective covers which were sewn in a mix of plain glazed chintzes and two co-ordinating prints. The main print features cameos of bush babies, such as koalas, cockatoos, wombats and platypuses, encircled with gum blossoms and wattle blooms. Its companion print has stripes defined by foliage, nuts and blossoms, with a koala or two for good measure. Strips between inside back and outside back were well suited to plain-colored boxing borders edged with piping. And the pleated skirt of the circular seated chair was well suited to the companion print.

MATERIALS

Child's cane chair

Sufficient print and companion print fabrics

Co-ordinating solid-colour fabric in 2 colours

Pencil

Scissors

Tape measure

Sheets of brown paper

Matching sewing thread

Narrow piping cord

Fusible wadding

5 buttons

COVER with PLEATED SKIRT

MAKING A PATTERN

Use fusible wadding to make the patterns for those pieces which will be backed with it. The wadding catches the fibers of the cane, which hold it in place, making it easier to work with than paper.

Inside back Fold the fusible wadding around the inside back of the chair. Trace the shape of this entire section onto the wadding. Cut out the pattern.

Seat   Make a pattern for the seat in the same manner.

Boxing strips   Use fusible wadding to make a pattern for the boxing strip at the seat front border. Make another pattern for the border strip between the inside back and outside back, extending it down to the bottom of the seat front border.

Left: One of the toddler-sized cane chairs.
Below: Teddy bears at ease on chairs with bush babies covers.

Outside back   Pin or tape brown paper to one half of the outside back from centre top to lower seat and around to the outer front of the chair. Carefully mark this shape on the paper with pencil. Add 2 cm (¾ in) all round for seams, and 10 cm (4 in) at the centre back for buttoning. Cut out the back pattern.

CUTTING OUT

Skirt The skirt is a double thickness of fabric with the vertically patterned companion print edged and lined with a plain chintz. Determine the length of the skirt and the width needed for pleating; 7.5 cm (3 in) wide box pleats correspond with pattern. Cut and piece sufficient fabric to make the pleated skirt, adding 2 cm (¾ in) for all seams. When cutting, cut the printed fabric 2.5 cm (1 in) shorter than the skirt length, and the solid color fabric 2.5 cm (1 in) longer.

Upper part of chair cover Lay the fusible wadding pieces on the fabric and cut out 2 cm (¾ in) beyond them. Cut seat from main print, centring motifs, the inside back from the companion print, and boxing strips from solid-colored fabric. Following manufacturer's instructions, fuse the wadding to the fabric. Cut two outside backs from main print. From a solid color, cut sufficient 4 cm (1½ in) wide bias strips for piping.

ASSEMBLING

Make sufficient piping before beginning. Join the bias strips for the desired length. Fold in half lengthwise and place the piping cord in the fold. With the zipper foot on your sewing machine, stitch the piping cord in place.

Attaching inside back to seat With a zipper foot, stitch piping around the seat and around the top and sides of the inside back. With right sides together and raw edges matching, stitch the inside back to the seat.

Back view of pleated skirt chair cover.

Attaching boxing strips Stitch the seat front boxing strip in place at the front of the seat. Stitch the remaining boxing strip around the edge of the inside back. Stitch piping along the remaining edge of the boxing strip.

Attaching outside back Narrow hem the centre back edges. Press 5 cm (2 in) to the wrong side at both centre backs and baste along the top edge in the seam allowance. With right sides together, pin the outside backs to the border boxing strip, aligning centres and overlapping the folded edges at the upper back. Check the fit on the chair, easing and making adjustments where necessary. The cover should fit snugly. Stitch the outside back to the border boxing strip, stitching as close to the piping as possible. With the zipper foot, stitch piping around the lower edge.

Making the skirt With right sides together and matching the raw edges, stitch the two skirt pieces together along one long side. Press seam flat and then press with raw edges matching to determine lower edge with band of plain color. Pin and stitch the two short ends together. Turn right side out and press. In the seam allowance of skirt top, baste along the raw edge to bond print with lining. Mark out pleats then pin, press and baste them in place.

Attaching skirt to seat With right sides together, pin the skirt to the lower edge of the upper chair cover assembly. Stitch in place with zipper foot as close to the piping cord as possible.

Finishing Mark and make buttonholes at the back. Stitch buttons in place to match the buttonholes. Overlock or zigzag all raw edges.

COVER with GATHERED SKIRT

When fusible wadding was pressed onto the inside back/seat/seat front of this chair, another plane was revealed – the inside arm. Wadding and then fabric pieces were cut for it and piping used to differentiate the inside arm from the single swoop of the principal cover piece. The gathered skirt starts at the lower inside edge of the boxing strip and is tacked to the lower corner of the seat front.

MATERIALS

Bias binding, in addition to the same materials for the cover with pleated skirt.

MAKING A PATTERN

Use fusible wadding to make the patterns for those pieces which will be backed with it.

Almost room for three.

Inside back/seat/seat front section Press the fusible wadding onto the inside back/seat seat. Draw the shape onto the wadding. Cut out the pattern.

Inside arms In the same manner, make a pattern for the inside arms with fusible wadding.

Boxing strips Use fusible wadding to make a pattern for the boxing strip between the inside back/inside arm and outside back of the chair.

Outside back Same as for cover with pleated skirt.

When making a pattern, folds in fusible wadding suggested the inside arm plane on this chair.

CUTTING OUT

Skirt Determine the length of the skirt and add 2 cm (¾ in) top and bottom for seam allowance and hem. Measure the distance between side of the seat front to the centre edge of the outside back – 66 cm (26 in) on this chair. Allow two and a half to three times this measurement plus hems and seams for gathering. Cut two skirt pieces from companion print.

Upper part of chair cover Lay the fusible wadding pieces on the fabric and cut out 2 cm (¾ in) beyond them. Cut the inside back/seat/seat front piece from main print, centring motifs. Cut the inside arm from the companion print and boxing strip from solid-colored fabric. Following manufacturer's instructions, fuse the wadding to the fabric. Cut two outside backs from the companion print. Cut sufficient 4 cm (1½ in) wide bias strips from a solid color for piping.

ASSEMBLING

Make sufficient piping before beginning. Join the bias strips for the desired length. Fold in half lengthwise, wrong sides together and place the piping cord in the fold. With the zipper foot on your sewing machine, baste the piping cord in place.

Attaching inside arms to inside back/seat/seat front section
With a zipper foot, stitch piping down the sides and around lower edge of inside back/seat/seat front piece. With right sides together, stitch this piece to inside arm pieces, stitching as close to the piping as possible. Stitch piping along the remaining edge of the inside arms and across the top of the piece for the inside back/seat/seat front.

Attaching boxing strip With right sides together, stitch the boxing strip in place close to the piped edge. With raw edges matching, stitch another row of piping on the remaining side of the boxing strip.

Attaching outside back Same as for cover with pleated skirt.

Attaching skirt Narrow hem the lower edge and both ends of each strip. Gather the upper edge. With right sides together, pin the skirt to the lower edges of the boxing strips and outside backs. Stitch in place as close to the piping as possible.

Finishing Stitch bias binding to the lower edge of seat front, as close to the piping as possible. Turn to the back and slip stitch in place. Tack skirt edge to side of seat front. Mark and make buttonholes at the back. Stitch buttons in place to match buttonholes. Overlock or zigzag all raw edges.

Right: Transformation that owes more to a cartoon character Tinkerbell than Titania. Below: Cane chair as a mere mortal.

FAIRY CHAIR

It is advisable to suspend all adult judgments regarding taste when faced with a child's choice for fabrics and trimmings. For this fairy chair, shocking pink was the inevitable choice with lots of shine, glitter, bows and frills.

Satin and tulle were the fabrics used and you'll find that it doesn't take much to convert a cane chair to a storybook throne. The fairy mantle is a satin slip cover with padded backrest and seat. The skirt is four layers of gathered and scalloped fabric; three tulle overskirts, graded in length, with a longer satin one underneath. White satin wings are stiffened with interfacing and padded with thick polyester wadding (batting).

The fusible wadding from which patterns are made becomes the padding for the seat, inside back and outside back. The outside back is sewn double but padded only at the top.

MATERIALS

Pink satin for seat
and back cover

White satin for wings

Pink tulle for skirt

Fusible wadding

Fabric marking pen

Thick polyester quilt
wadding (batting)

Heavy interfacing

Purchased pink piping (or
self-piping from pink satin)

Gold and silver glitter
fabric paints

Pink velvet ribbon

Velcro®

Self-adhesive stars

Glue (from glue gun or
a fabric to timber glue)

Pencil

Brown paper

Matching sewing thread

Seam tape

MAKING PATTERNS

Use fusible wadding to make patterns for inside back, outside back and seat. Place it on the chair – the cane will generally catch the fibres on the back of the wadding. Use tape or pins to hold it in place if necessary. Measure finished sizes on fusible wadding. Seam allowance is added when cutting fabric.

Inside back and outside back Hold fusible wadding against the outside back of the chair and, with pencil, carefully mark on it the shape of the chair to the lower edge of seat. If the top is wider than the seat, widen the sides so the cover will slip easily onto the chair. Cut away outside back and use this as a guide to cut an inside back pattern, noting that the length for the inside back extends only to the top of the seat.

Seat If your seat, like this one, is concave, you will need to make a cushion to fill it in. Use calico and then stuff with fibrefill. Make seat pattern from fusible wadding and cut out.

Wings Fold the brown paper in half. With a pencil and, using the photo as a guide, make a pattern for the wings. They are oval, finished size 33 cm (13 in) by 30 cm (12 in), with a gash in each outside edge and connected in the centre by a 10 cm (4 in) band. You may need to experiment a few times until you are satisfied with the result.

Skirt Decide on skirt length and add a 2 cm (¾ in) seam allowance. Skirt length for this chair is 28 cm (11 in). To determine the width, measure around the front and sides of the chair (this chair measures 92 cm or 36 in) and double this measurement. You may need to join widths of fabric to make the skirt.

CUTTING OUT

Pink satin Measure and cut the required widths for the skirt adding 2 cm (¾ in) for seams where necessary. Mark two strips each 20 cm x 35 cm (8 in x 14 in) for the bows. Lay the inside back, outside back and seat pieces cut in fusible wadding on the fabric. Use fabric marker to draw a straight skirt ending 5 cm (2 in) above the floor – the lower edge of the outside back. Cut out all pieces, cutting 2 cm (¾ in) beyond the fusible wadding. Cut an extra back. Following the manufacturer's instructions, fuse the wadding to one of the outside backs, the inside back and seat.

White satin Cut two pairs of wings.

Interfacing Cut four wings minus the centre band, and 1.2 cm (½ in) smaller all round.

Thick wadding Cut a pair of wings the same size as interfacing wings.

Three layers of tulle with the scalloped satin skirt are stitched to the seat.

Tulle Cut three skirts, each 10 cm (4 in), 15 cm (6 in), and 20 cm (8 in) long, and the same width as the satin skirt.

Making skirt scallops

Concertina-fold the satin skirt into equal sections about 20 cm (8 in) wide. Pin or tape them together, then trim away each side of lower edge of folded fabric to make a large scallop. Unfold the fabric. Repeat with each tulle skirt layer. Finish all the scallops of the satin skirt with a closely-spaced narrow zigzag stitch. Finish the scalloped edges of the tulle skirts in the same manner.

Painting

Following the manufacturer's instructions, paint gold and silver stars and moons on the front of the wings, the inside back of the chair, and on each scallop of the satin skirt. Allow to dry thoroughly.

ASSEMBLING

Attaching the inside back to outside back With right sides together, pin the two outside backs together. Stitch them together around the edges below the section of fused wadding. Turn right side out and press. With a zipper foot, stitch piping around the top and sides of the inside back. Pin inside back to outside back, right sides together, starting from the centre. Continue pinning down each side. Check the fit on the chair, easing and making adjustments where necessary. The cover should slip easily onto the chair. Stitch the inside back and outside back together with the zipper foot, stitching as close to the piping as possible.

Attaching seat to inside back Stitch piping around the seat, same as for inside back. With right sides together, pin the rear of the seat to the lower edge of the inside back and stitch.

Attaching skirt to seat Place the three tulle skirts and the satin skirt together in layers. Mark the centre of the top edge. Gather all the layers together to fit the front and sides of the seat by machine or hand, matching the centre of the skirt with the centre of the seat front. Using zipper foot and with right sides together and raw edges matching, stitch the skirt in place as close as possible to the piping on the seat. Overlock or finish all raw edges with machine zigzag stitch. With needle and thread to match the skirt, catch tulle layers to satin skirt in the centres of the scallops at the front.

Making wings Place the wadding inside the two layers of interfacing. Stitch together close to the raw edges. With right sides together, stitch the satin wings together, leaving an opening in the centre of the lower edge of each wing. Turn to right side and press with a cool iron. Insert the interfacing wings through the openings and slip stitch them closed.

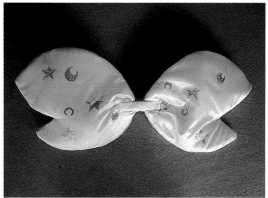

Velcro® is attached to the centre back of wings.

Attaching wings Stitch a strip of the loop side of the Velcro® to the centre back of the wings. Stitch two small pieces at the top edge of the wings, at a position where they can attach to the cover. Place the cover on the chair, position the wings on outside back of chair, and mark the Velcro® placement on the outside back to correspond with that of the wings. Remove the cover and stitch the hook side of the Velcro® in place.

Making bows Fold the strips in half lengthwise, right sides together. Stitch along the side and each end, leaving an opening in the long side for turning. Turn right side out and slip stitch the opening closed. Press. Fold the strips into bows and tie the centres with several strands of thread. Stitch in place at the sides of the chair.

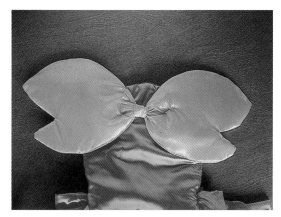

Wings in place on the outside back.

Feet Glue the velvet ribbon in place around the lower edge of each leg. When dry, wind the ribbon around the legs, winding as high as necessary to cover any visible legs. Glue the remaining end in place. Stick self-adhesive stars to the ribbon.

Ties Cut a 45 cm (18 in) length of seam tape. Fold it in half and stitch it to the underside of the centre front of the seat seam. Place the cover on the chair, and tie the cover in place.

TWO-TOWEL LOUNGE

Abeach-themed loose cover for a toddler's foam lounge can be quickly stitched from two shell-bordered towels. One towel is sufficient to cover the seat and back rest. The other is cut in two for the sides. The face cloths were just the right size for flanged covers for the tiny cushions.

ASSEMBLING
If you have an overlocker (serger), use it for this project. Even good quality towels have a tendency to fray when they have been cut, so take care to finish all cut edges.

Seat and Back Rest
Lay a towel, wrong side out, across the lounge from front to back, beginning and ending with a small overhang on the floor. If your towel has a border, position it close to the lower edge and match it to the border of the sides. Tuck the remainder in the crevice behind the seat.

Above: Toddler-sized foam lounge.
Right: Cover materials – two bath towels and two face cloths.
Next page: Comfortable cover is quickly cut and sewn from two towels.

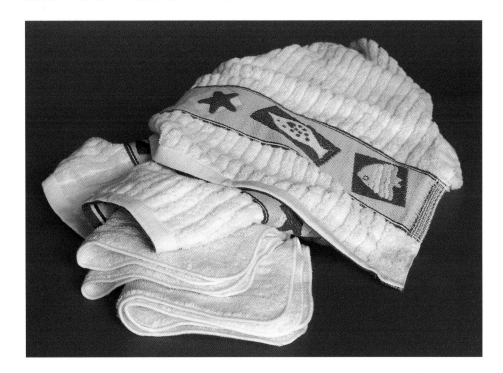

MATERIALS

Toddler's foam lounge
2 full size bath towels
2 face cloths
Small amount calico
Scissors
Tape measure
Fabric marker
Matching sewing thread
Elastic

Arms

Cut the remaining towel in half crosswise. Place the towel halves, wrong side out, over each arm, matching borders with the front and back. Pin them together at the rear and the front, taking in the seam up the inside front of the arm and across the top front of the arm. Remove the cover and sew the pinned seams. Replace the cover, again with the wrong side out. Pin the inside arms to the seat and the inside back, trimming the excess towel as you work. Pleat and pin any excess at the outer joins of the arms and back rest. Remove the cover and stitch the pinned seams. Clip into the seam allowance where necessary. Finish all seams and raw edges.

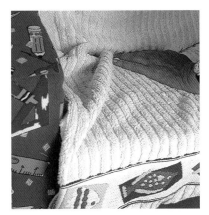

Fitting the first towel over the seat and back rest.

Making pleat to cope with the excess where back rest joins arm.

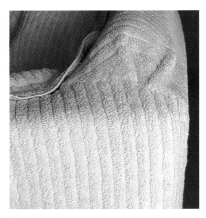

Detail of the pleat at the outer arm/back rest join.

Fitting and pinning the inside arm seams on the wrong side.

Elasticising the Base

Place the cover on the lounge, still wrong side out. Pin a hem on the lower edge overhang. Turn lounge over. Pin darts in each corner of the underside so the base will sit flat. Remove the cover and stitch hem and darts. Turn cover to right side and place on the lounge. Thread elastic through the casing on the towel, making small snips in the casing at each corner to bring the elastic out and into the casing on the adjacent side.

Cushion Covers

Cut two pieces of calico the size of the cushions, plus 1 cm (³⁄₈ in) all round. Press the seam allowances to the wrong side on all edges of the calico. Centre the calico on the back of the face washer, with wrong sides together. Stitch the calico in place, leaving an opening in the centre of one side. Insert the cushion, then close the opening with machine stitching.

BEE CHAIR

A coat of paint and a new, hand-stencilled cover greatly revived this child-sized iron-framed chair. Three stencils of the bee motif were cut in clear acetate film – one for the wings, one for the black parts of the body and another for the yellow stripes on the abdomen. For the inside back, the hive was stencilled in turquoise with the simple doorway and swarm details painted on later in black.

Above: Rusted frame and worn fabric of the chair. Right: Freshly upholstered with stencils of hive and swarm on the back and bees in flight on the seat.

MATERIALS

Emery paper
Paint brush
Rust retardant
Undercoat
Gloss paint, turquoise
Strong cotton fabric
such as canvas
Pencil
Fine black felt pen
Clear acetate film
Scalpel or small craft knife
Adhesive tape
Self-healing cutting board
or several sheets of old
cardboard
Fabric paints in turquoise,
black and yellow
Stiff bristle-haired brush
Small sable-haired brush
Screwdriver
Spray-on dirt-repellent
preparation
Polyester wadding
(batting)
Spray adhesive
Tacks
Hammer

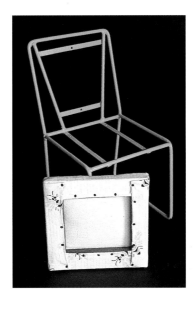

Painting Frame

Unscrew the back and seat from the frame. Prise away tacks, remove original covers and reserve for patterns. Determine extent of upholstery repairs. Here, only one layer of polyester wadding was smoothed over the existing padding.

Sand the frame and paint it with rust retardant following manufacturer's instructions for numbers of coats and drying time. Paint with undercoat and after recommended drying time, finish with gloss paint. Two or more coats always give a superior finish.

Making Stencils

Cut the acetate into small sheets and with black felt pen, trace over bee motif three times and hive motif once. Motifs are reproduced same size on page 141. Trace whole bee motifs each time to help with the alignment of images on the fabric.

Steady the sheet of acetate film on layered cardboard or self-healing cutting board with adhesive tape. Using a scalpel, cut out stencils to correspond with appropriate colours.

Stencilling Fabric

Cut new fabric pieces generously from the old upholstery.

Determine placement of bee motifs. On this chair, the design starts in the centre of the seat with the bee 'flying' towards a front corner. One in front and one behind are also headed in this direction. Although they do fly in a straight line, they are about 15° off course on both sides of the front-to-back centre line. The others are angled towards the other front corner. This was deliberately done in order to give the fabric a random, non-repeating pattern.

Top of page: Back of seat and painted frame.
Above: Fabric and stencils. Acetate stencils instead of the cardboard ones shown here, aid alignment of motifs on fabric.

Plot the motifs on the fabric and then, with pencil and the stencil designated for the black paint, lightly draw around the stencil parts onto the fabric. These pencil marks will eventually be covered by the black paint.

Practise stencilling on a scrap of fabric before filling in the motifs on the fabric. Start with the lightest color (in this case the turquoise) and use the appropriate stencil carefully placed over the drawn-in black bits of the bee.

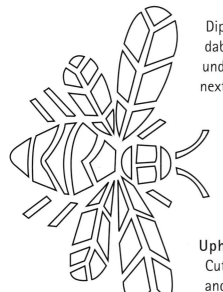

Dip the tip of the stiff-bristle brush into turquoise fabric paint and dab the color onto the fabric. Lift stencil away carefully, wipe the underside of the stencil clean and then re-align the stencil on the next motif. Clean brush thoroughly before moving to the next color and then finish with the black. Allow fabric to dry and follow manufacturer's instructions for setting the paint; some recommend that heat from a hot iron will do the trick.

Stencil the hive onto the centre of the back. With black fabric paint, and using sable brush, paint on door and dots to represent the swarm of bees. Allow to dry and set as above.

Upholstering Chair
Cut pieces of polyester wadding the same size as the chair seat and back. Slope edges with scissors and attach to seat and back with spray adhesive.

Above: Bee stencil.
Right: Hive stencil.

For seat Centre fabric on seat, turn fabric and seat over and tack excess to the underside of the centre front of seat. Stretch to centre back and tack in place. Centre and tack to the sides in this manner. Then work out to the corners, folding excess under neatly and tacking in place.

For back Centre fabric on back, turn fabric and back over together and tack excess to the underside of centre top of back. Stretch down to centre bottom of back and tack in place. Centre and tack to the sides in this manner. Then work out to the corners, folding excess under and tacking in place to neaten corners.

Spray upholstery with dirt-repellent preparation and when completely dry, screw back and seat onto frame.

141

QUICK RECOVERY

DOTTY SOFA

Masses of ruffled, red-dotted fabric give a flamboyant character to a lackluster brown three-seater. The ruffling adds body to the mean proportions of the piece and also provides a short cut to fitting and seaming. The only panels cut to fit accurately on the cover are on the seat and the fronts of the arms. The arms and back 'flow' over various awkward planes and angles. There was plenty of fabric to play with –

MATERIALS

Sofa
Sufficient fabric
Small amount of
co-ordinating fabric
for the legs
Scissors
Pins
Tape measure
Fabric marker
Matching sewing thread
Ruffling foot
Jumbo rickrack
Co-ordinating piping
Staple gun

Opposite top: Thirty something three-seater with its original brown wool/mix upholstery. Right: Revived with ruffled dotty fabric, rickrack and bright legs and cushions.

30 yards in all of a bargain-priced polyester/cotton sheeting – and there is still masses left over. The beauty of having so much fabric is that you can drape, stitch and then cut away the excess. Originally I was going to make this a loose cover, but it seemed much quicker and easier to staple it to the underside of the frame. The idea of this project was to extend the life of an unremarkable piece of furniture by a couple of years as cheaply and quickly as possible. The sofa was finished in less than a day.

CUTTING OUT

Remove the cushions from the sofa. Cut a seat the same size as the existing seat. Pin it in place and, using the seat as a guide, measure and cut the pieces.

Using the original cushion covers as a guide, cut the required number of cushion tops and bottoms. Cut a long strip of fabric for the boxing strip the width of the original strip plus 2.5 cm (1 in) seam allowance. The length will depend on the ruffler settings.

ASSEMBLING

Test the ruffling foot and adjust to the desired amount of ruffle. A ruffling foot will ruffle a single layer of fabric, as well as ruffling an upper layer of fabric and stitching it to a flat lower layer of fabric beneath the foot. Follow the manufacturer's instructions. If you do not have a ruffling foot, gather fabric by zigzag stitching over dental floss (see page 66), then pull the fabric up along the dental floss to gather it. Take care that the needle does not catch the dental floss. Machine stitch over the gathers to hold them.

Back

Fabric here was wide enough to reach from the rear of the seat, over the inside back and down the outside back to the floor. If necessary, join two pieces for the inside back and outside back at the top edge. Using the ruffling foot with right sides of fabric together and the seat piece underneath, join one long edge of the fabric

143

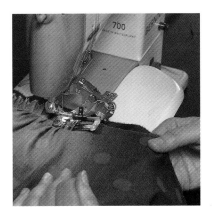

Although it appears unwieldy at first, a ruffling attachment is brilliant for pleating and gathering.

Arm cover prior to attaching it to seat, back and front panel.

Seat cushions take shape; ruffled boxing strip, piped top with bottom marked for piping.

(railroaded) to the seat, allowing about 10 cm (4 in) to extend beyond the seat at each end. Place the seat on the sofa and, with tailor's chalk, mark the centre of the top border between inside back and outside back. Remove the cover and ruffle along this line. Stitch rickrack over the ruffling stitches and arrange on sofa.

Lower Front
In the same way as for the back, ruffle and stitch a railroaded length of fabric along the front edge of the seat platform. Trim the fabric to floor level.

Arms
Drape fabric across the arm with one raw edge on the floor and tear or cut it at the seat, allowing a generous seam. Determine the centre line of the border between inside and outside arm. Ruffle along this line and then stitch rickrack over the ruffling stitches and arrange on sofa. Repeat for the other arm.

Cut two rectangles of fabric for the front panels of the arm, the depth to the floor and twice the width. Ruffle along the top edge. Place the arms on the sofa with their wrong sides out and pin the arm fronts in place. Remove and stitch.

Align the front of seat with beginning of inside arm. Using ruffling attachment and with right sides together and the seat piece underneath, ruffle the inside arm to the seat.

Then sew the seam at the front panel and the lower part of the arm front panel, right sides together.

Attaching Arms to Inside Back and Outside Back
Place cover on sofa, wrong side out. To close the gap above the back of the arm at the back side border, pin the inside back to the outside back – the fullness from the ruffling on top will accommodate this.

Red piped cushions have ruffled boxing strips.

Then pin the outside back to the outside arm and inside back to the inside arm above the back corner of the seat. Remove the cover and stitch.

Cushions

With right sides together and matching raw edges, stitch piping around the seat cushion pieces with a zipper foot. With the ruffling foot, ruffle both long edges of the boxing strip. With a zipper foot, stitch the boxing strip to the cushion top, then to the cushion bottom, leaving an opening along most of the back side of the bottom. Turn right side out, insert the cushion and slip stitch the opening closed. If desired, you can insert zippers into the seam at the lower back.

Legs

Remove the floor protectors from the legs of the sofa. Cut a strip of fabric to fit around the leg and stitch the right sides of this piece together to

Bright pink chintz 'socks' were made for the legs of the sofa.

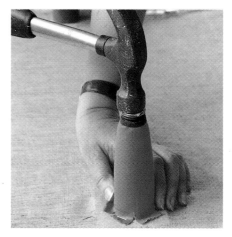

With fabric in place, floor protectors are tapped back on the legs.

make a sleeve. Turn to right side and press. Place the sleeve on the leg. Snip into the upper edge, and staple to the base of the sofa with a staple gun. Ensuring the raw edges of the fabric are turned in and hidden, replace the floor protectors.

Finishing
Place the cover on the sofa and make any necessary adjustments. Pin the cover to the sofa at close and regular intervals around the lower edge. Turn the sofa over and staple the ends of the cover to the underside of the frame, ensuring the gathers are evenly distributed around the cover.

THROW PILLOWS

MATERIALS
Sufficient fabric
Scissors
Pins
Tape measure
Pencil
Brown paper
30 cm (12 in) plate
Fabric marker
Matching sewing thread
Ruffling foot
Co-ordinating piping
Size 16 (40 cm/16 in)
  cushion inserts
Polyester fibrefill

Components for the circular cushions.

CUTTING OUT
For the round pillows, use the plate as a template and draw a circle on brown paper. Cut two from the fabric. Cut a 15 cm (6 in) boxing strip about three times the circumference of the circle. For the triangular pillows, on brown paper draw an isosceles triangle with the base 40 cm (16 in) and the other two sides each measuring 38 cm (15 in). Cut two from the fabric. Cut a 10 cm (4 in) boxing strip three times the circumference of the triangle.

ASSEMBLING
Boxing Strip
With the ruffling foot, ruffle along both long sides of the boxing strip, stitching close to the raw edges.

Cushion
Matching raw edges, stitch the piping to the cushion front and back. Cut the boxing strip to fit around the front of the pillow, plus 2 cm (¾ in). Stitch the short ends of the boxing strip together to form a loop. Pin it in place, matching the raw edges. Stitch the boxing strip in place. Stitch the cushion back to the boxing strip, leaving an opening for turning. Turn right side out. Place the pillow insert inside the pillow, or stuff with fibrefill. Slip stitch the opening closed.

LIFE ON THE LOOSE

E̲xtravagant costumes reveal the pantomime personalities locked in a pair of very sensible chairs. The graceful lines of a Fritz Hansen moulded ply-wood design respond sensuously to a daring frilled flamenco cover. The Louis XVI-style chair with its skeletal back and padded seat has a multi-patterned cover which Bo Peep might covet. The striped underskirt is slightly gathered and banded in black at the bottom. Over this is a plaid confection, fringed and lined with the spotted fabric of the top, which is pleated part way along the back sash. To show more of the stripes, the plaid skirt is hitched up at the corners like an Austrian blind.

Above: Naked molded plywood chair.
Right: Flamboyant covers with frills and fringing.

BLUE and YELLOW CHAIR COVER

Sufficient print, stripe
and plaid fabrics
Sufficient black fabric
Fringe trimming
4 tufts to match fringe
(to make, see Winter
Palace, page 122)
Pencil
Scissors
Tape measure
Sheets of brown paper
Fabric marker
Matching sewing thread
String to make very
narrow piping cord

MAKING A PATTERN

Outside back Pin or tape brown paper to the outside back of the chair and mark the shape of the chair back to upper seat height on the paper with a pencil. Align the lower edges of the side of the pattern with the widest part of the chair, so the cover will slip on without any openings. Add 3 cm (1¼ in) all round for seams and ease, then cut out the outside back pattern.

Inside back Cut the inside back the same as the outside back, leaving extra paper at the seat edge. Pin or tape the pattern to the inside front of the chair, mark at the seat then add 2 cm (¾ in) along the seat edge and cut out.

Seat Pin or tape the paper to the seat. Trace the seat shape onto the paper, add 2 cm (¾ in) all round for seams and cut out.

Striped skirt To determine the depth of the skirt, measure from slightly above the floor to the edge of the seat and add a 2 cm (¾ in) seam. To determine the width of the skirt strip, measure around the front, sides and back of the chair and add a metre (one yard). You may have to join fabric widths to make the skirt.

CUTTING OUT

Cut the outside back, inside back and seat pieces from the print fabric. Mark the necessary rectangular shapes for the skirt directly onto the striped fabric with a fabric marker, adding 2 cm (¾ in) for seams between each panel (if necessary) and cut out. From the plaid fabric, cut a 45 cm x 2.75 m (17¾ in x 3 yd 1 in) upper skirt. You will have to join fabric strips to do this. From the print fabric, cut the same size lining and a 25 cm x 1.4 m (10 in x 55 in) sash. From the black fabric, cut a 28 cm x 1.4 m (11 in x 55 in) sash lining, a hem binding strip 6 cm (2½ in) wide x the width of the striped skirt. On the straight grain, cut sufficient black piping strips to go around the seat front and sides and all around the back seam of the chair, 5 cm (2 in) wide.

ASSEMBLING

Make sufficient piping before beginning. Join the strips for the desired length. Fold in half lengthwise and place the string in the fold. With the zipper foot on your sewing machine, baste the string in place.

Attaching Seat to Inside Back

With right sides together, pin the seat panel to the lower edge of the inside back panel. Stitch in place.

Attaching Inside Back and Outside Back

With the zipper foot on your sewing machine, stitch piping around the sides and top of the outside back and around the front and sides of the seat. With right sides together, pin the outside back to the inside back, matching the centres. Continue pinning down each side. Check the fit on the chair, easing and making adjustments where necessary. The cover should fit around the upper edges, and slip easily onto the chair. Stitch the inside back and outside back together, stitching close to the piping.

Attaching Striped Skirt to Seat

Join the skirt pieces with 2 cm (¾ in) seams to form a loop. Mark the upper edge into four equal quarters. On one long edge of the hem binding, press 1 cm (⅜ in) to the wrong side. With right sides together and matching the raw edges, pin the unpressed edge of the binding to the lower edge of the skirt. Stitch the binding in place 1.2 cm (½ in) from the edge. Turn the binding to the wrong side and stitch in place by hand or machine. Gather the upper edge to fit the seat piece by machine or hand, matching the marked quarters with the corners. Stitch in place as close to the cord of the piping as possible. Overlock or zigzag all raw edges.

Making Plaid Upper Skirt

With right sides together, stitch the plaid upper skirt and print lining together with a 1 cm (⅜ in) seam around all four sides. Leave an opening in the centre of one end for turning. Turn right side out and press. Stitch the fringe along one long side and both ends.

Attaching Plaid Upper Skirt

Place the cover on the chair. Matching the centre of the upper skirt with the centre front of the seat, pin the skirt to the cover over the striped skirt and flush with the piping. At both front corners, make inverted pleats about 5 cm (2 in) wide. Continue pinning around both sides to the back corners of the chair. Make inverted pleats at these corners as for the front and leave the remainder of the skirt hanging. Remove the cover and with a zipper foot, top stitch the skirt in place around the front and both sides as close as possible to the piping. (The piping will cover this line of stitching.) Along the upper unattached ends of the plaid skirt, pin even pleats about 2.5 cm (1 in) wide to make each of these sections about 20 cm (8 in) long. Baste across the pleats close to the top edge.

Overleaf: Back view of the blue and yellow cover shows how the pleated ends of the plaid skirt are attached to the sash.

Making Sash

With right sides together and matching raw edges, stitch the sash and sash lining together with a 1 cm (⅜ in) seam along both long edges. Turn right side out and press, arranging an equal amount of lining visible on each side. Press the ends 1 cm (⅜ in) to the inside and top stitch.

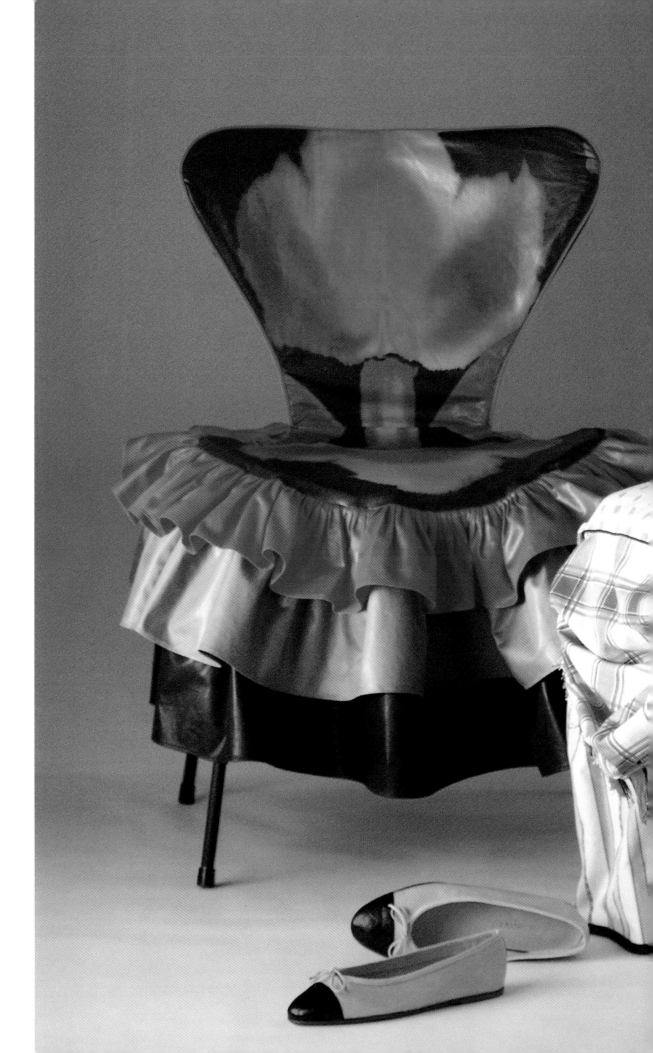

Attaching Sash
Place the cover on the chair. With the sash lining against the right side of the inside back, match the centre of the sash with the centre of the inside back and wrap the ends of the sash loosely around to the outside back of the chair. Pin the sash to the side seams of the inside back and outside back. Pin the pleated sections from the upper edge of the plaid skirt to the sash, beginning at the side seam and pinning towards the ends of the sash. Remove the cover and top stitch the pleats to the underside of the sash. Remove the pins at the sides. The sash is only connected to the cover at the pleats of upper skirt.

Finishing Upper Skirt
With a needle and double thread and starting at the lower edge, make running stitches at the centre of each pleated corner and gather up the fabric to about 15 cm (6 in) long. Secure the threads. Stitch purchased or homemade tufts over pleated corners with black thread. Place the cover on the chair and tie the sash loosely at the outside back.

FLAMENCO COVER

MATERIALS
Sufficient fabric in print, coral, green and black
Pencil
Scissors
Tape measure
Sheets of brown paper
Fabric marker
Matching sewing thread
10 small black eyelets
Narrow piping cord
5 cm (2 in) black Velcro®

MAKING A PATTERN
Inside back and outside back Tape brown paper to the outside back of the chair and carefully mark the shape of the chair to the bend of the seat on the paper with a pencil. Add 2 cm (³⁄₄ in) to all edges for seams and ease, then cut out the inside back pattern. For the outside back pattern, fold the inside back in half, and trace around it again, then add 12 cm (4½ in) for the centre outside back facing.

Seat Pin or tape the paper to the seat and trace the seat shape onto it. Add 2 cm (³⁄₄ in) all round for seams and cut out.

Skirt Cut ruffle strips as listed below, joining lengths as necessary.

CUTTING OUT
Cut an inside back and two outside backs, and one seat from print fabric. Take care to match prints if necessary. From black, cut a ruffle strip 35 cm x 4 m 35 cm (13½ in x 3 yd 28 in) and a 2.5 cm x 115 cm (1 in x 45 in) tie. Cut a green strip 24 cm x 4 m 35 cm (9½ in x 3 yd 28 in). From coral, cut a 14 cm x 4 m 35 cm (5½ in x 3 yd 28 in) ruffle strip and a 5 cm (2 in) wide bias strip to go around the sides and top of the inside back.

ASSEMBLING

Attaching Seat to Inside Back

With right sides together, pin the rear seam of the seat to the lower edge of the inside back. Stitch them together.

Attaching Inside Back and Outside Back

Press 4 cm (1½ in) to the wrong side twice along centre edges of both outside back pieces. Stitch in place. Fold the piping strip in half, place the piping cord inside the fold and with zipper foot on machine, stitch as close as possible to the cord. Matching raw edges, stitch the piping to the right side of the inside back. With right sides together, pin the outside back and inside back together. Check the fit on the chair, making adjustments where necessary. The cover should fit snugly. Stitch together with a zipper foot, stitching as close to the piping as possible.

Making Skirt

Narrow hem along one long edge of each ruffle strip. At both short ends, press 2 cm (¾ in) to the wrong side twice and stitch hems in place. Measure from the centre outside back around the edge of the seat and return to the centre outside back and add 6 cm (2½ in). Gather each ruffle to this length by machine or hand.

Attaching Skirt to Seat

Layer the ruffles on top of each other with the raw gathered edges matching. Baste the ruffles together. With right sides together, pin the ruffles to the seat, starting at the centre outside back and working around, with 6 cm (2½ in) extending beyond the other centre outside back. Stitch in place. Overlock or zigzag all raw edges.

Finishing

Fold the tie strip in half lengthwise. Stitch along the raw edges and turn right side out. Insert eyelets at 6 cm (2½ in) intervals along both sides of the centre outside back, 1.2 cm (½ in) in from the edges. To hold the skirt ends together: just below the back opening, stitch the loop piece of Velcro® in place at the inner top edge of the black ruffle, and the hook piece of Velcro® to correspond with it at the beginning of the 6 cm (2½ in) extension of the coral ruffle. Place the cover on the chair and lace it up.

Above: Spoonback chair
in a more subdued mood.
Right: Close-fitting
covers in dramatic black
and white prints.

GRAPHIC DISTINCTIONS

Because of their easy elegance, modern spoon-backs are the darlings of interior designers and diners alike. Slip these same chairs into skin tight covers emblazoned with boldly brushed bands, twisted cords and trick-question symbolism and they acquire a kind of wrought iron edginess. But the eye is not fooled for long; we are quickly consoled by the pleasant proportions and comfortable curves which are, after all, only crisply defined in eye-catching black and white prints. Motifs have been deliberately positioned for maximum impact and darts and zips ensure a close fit.

BLACK and WHITE COVER with LONG SKIRT

MATERIALS
Sufficient fabric in
plain and in two other
graphic patterns
Wide black
grosgrain ribbon
Pencil
Scissors
Tape measure
Sheets of brown paper
Fabric marker
Matching sewing thread
Narrow piping cord
40 cm (16 in) zip fastener
5 cm (2 in) Velcro®

MAKING A PATTERN
Outside Back
Pin or tape brown paper to outside back of chair and carefully mark chair back shape to lower seat height with pencil. Add 2 cm (¾ in) all round for seams, then cut out the outside back pattern.

Inside Back
Pin or tape brown paper to inside back of chair. Fold paper around the sides and trace shape of chair, including sides, onto paper. At both top corners make three small darts in the paper so pattern fits shape of chair; these will be stitched down so the inside back conforms to the shape of the padded surface. Add extra fabric to seam between the front and the seat if necessary. Add 2 cm (¾ in) all round for seams, then cut out the pattern.

Seat
Pin or tape paper to seat. At both front corners make a dart in the paper so it fits the shape of the seat down to its lower edge; dart will be stitched to form the corners. Add extra fabric to seam between the inside back and the seat if necessary. Trace the seat shape down to the lower edge of the seat onto the paper and add 2 cm (¾ in) all round for seams and cut out.

Skirt

Measure from slightly above the floor to the lower edge of the seat. Add 5 cm (2 in) for the bottom hem and a 2 cm (¾ in) seam for the top of the skirt. To determine the width, measure around the front, sides and back of the chair. Add a total of 1.68 m (66 in) for the four inverted pleats at each corner of the skirt and 2 cm (¾ in) for seams and hems. The skirt is not joined at the outside back in the return of the pleat below the zip fastening; Velcro® will keep the opening closed here. Note that the back panel is plain and the extra fabric in the inverted pleats is also plain. To achieve this configuration, you will need to join fabric for the skirt.

CUTTING OUT

Mark the required rectangular shapes for the skirt directly onto the fabric with a fabric marker, making allowance for pattern placement and adding 2 cm (¾ in) for seams at joins if necessary. Lay the outside back, inside back and seat pieces on the fabric. Cut out all pieces. Cut sufficient 4 cm (1½ in) wide bias strips for piping.

ASSEMBLING

Inside Back Shaping Darts

Place inside back on the chair, wrong side up. In each corner, pin three small darts to define the corner, taking care that they are even in size and position. Sew the darts.

Attaching Inside Back and Outside Back

Join the bias strips for the required lengths of piping for the back and seat. Fold in half lengthwise, place the piping cord in the fold and stitch with zipper foot as close as possible to the cord. Still with the zipper foot, stitch the piping around the sides and top of the inside back. With right sides together, pin outside back to inside back along the top, matching centres. Place assembly on chair, wrong side out, and continue pinning down each side. Establish the opening for the zipper, finger press the opening and release pins. Stitch the inside back and outside back together, stitching as close to the cord as possible and inserting zipper at the same time.

Seat Corner Darts

Place the seat fabric on the chair, wrong side out. At each front corner, pin a dart to define the corner so the seat fits snugly on the chair. Make darts even in size and position. Sew the darts.

Attaching Seat to Inside Back

Stitch piping around the sides and front of lower edge of seat with raw edges matching. With right sides together and raw edges matching, position and pin the rear edge of the seat to the lower edge of the inside back. Stitch together.

Inverted Pleats in Skirt

Join the skirt pieces with 2 cm (¾ in) seams to form one long piece. Narrow hem both short ends; these will be in the return of the inverted pleat below the zip on the outside back. Begin pinning the skirt onto the chair, wrong side out, from the point below the zip on the right-hand side of the outside back. At this point turn under 10.5 cm (4⅛ in) from the short end and align the fold with this corner. Work across the outside back to the next corner and mark the fabric. At this point, measure 42 cm (16½ in) further on along the top of the skirt and mark. Pin these two marked points with right sides together. Open out the pleat, distributing the excess evenly on either side of the corner, remove from chair and press flat. Pin and baste in place. Repeat for the other pleats, checking the fit on the chair at each corner. Back at the opening, one quarter of the pleat allowance has already been pinned in place at the beginning. Pin the other half of the pleat down the last side to be pinned and let the remaining back flap hang free.

Attaching Skirt to Seat

With right sides together and raw edges matching, pin the skirt to the seat, starting at the centre front and working out, and matching the pleats with each corner. Stitch in place as close to the piping cord as possible, allowing the last remaining flap of the pleat below the opening to hang free.

Finishing

Overlock or zigzag all raw edges. Stitch loop side of Velcro® to top outer face of last pleat flap and stitch hook side of Velcro® to corresponding point on wrong side of lower edge of seat.

Cut lengths of ribbon, fold in half and stitch to the tops of inverted pleats at rear corners as shown.

BLACK and WHITE COVER
with SHORT SKIRT

MATERIALS

Same as for other black and white chair cover.

MAKING A PATTERN

Outside back Same as for previous black and white cover.

Inside back Same as for previous black and white cover.

Seat Pin or tape paper to the seat and trace the upper seat shape onto it. Add 2 cm (¾ in) all round for seams and cut out. Measure the depth necessary for the boxing strip for seat border. To determine the length, measure around the front of the seat and both sides and add 4 cm (1½ in) for seams.

Skirt Because the skirt is sewn as a double thickness of fabric, decide on the length of the skirt, add 2 cm (¾ in) for top seam allowance and double

the total length. To determine the width, measure around the front, sides and back of the chair. Add 1.68 m (66 in) in total for the four inverted corner pleats of the skirt and 4 cm (1½ in) for seams.

CUTTING OUT

Mark out the skirt and boxing strip for seat border directly onto the fabric with a fabric marker, adding 2 cm (¾ in) for seams to piece the skirt where necessary. Lay the outside back, inside back and seat pieces on the fabric. Cut out all pieces. Cut sufficient 4 cm (1½ in) wide bias strips for piping, noting that the back, seat top and boxing strip are all piped.

ASSEMBLING

Inside Back Corner Darts

Place the inside back on the chair, wrong side up. In each corner pin three small darts to define the corner, taking care that they are even in size and position. Sew the darts.

Attaching Inside Back and Outside Back

Join the bias strips for the required length. Fold in half lengthwise, place the piping cord in the fold and stitch with zipper foot as close as possible to the cord. Still with the zipper foot, stitch piping around the sides and top of the inside back. With right sides together, pin outside back to the inside back along the top, matching the centres. Place assembly on chair, wrong side out, and continue pinning down each side. Establish the opening for the zipper, finger press the opening and release pins. Stitch the inside back and outside back together, stitching as close to the cord as possible and inserting zipper at the same time.

Seat and Border Boxing Strip

Following the directions above, make sufficient piping for the seat top and the lower edge of boxing strip. Place the seat fabric piece on the chair, match centre of seat front with centre front of fabric and pin piping around sides and front, raw edges matching. Stitch piping in place using zipper foot. Stitch piping to lower edge of border boxing strip, raw edges matching. With right sides together and raw edges matching, stitch border boxing strip to piped edge of seat top as close as possible to the piping cord.

Attaching Seat to Inside Back

With right sides together, pin the seat panel to the lower edge of the inside back. Stitch in place.

Inverted Pleats in Skirt

Join the skirt pieces with 2 cm (¾ in) seams to form one long piece. Fold this piece in half lengthwise and press. Then continue as in the last three steps for black and white cover with long skirt, but attaching grosgrain ribbon at tops of inverted pleats at the front corners and at the centre of outside back.

Back view of chairs.

MATERIALS

Screwdriver
Phillips head screwdriver
Allen keys
Self-sealing plastic bags
Labels
Stitch ripper
White marking pencil
Medium felt-tipped pen
Sufficient fabric for cover
Paper-backed fusible web
Fusible wadding (batting)
Scrap of thin foam
Scrap of polyester fibrefill
Stranded embroidery floss
in selected colours
2 embroidery needles
Embroidery hoop
Thimble
Scissors (embroidery
and large)
Matching thread
Staple gun
Curved needle
Invisible nylon thread

Above: Chair in its
original uninspiring
oatmeal wool cover.
Right: New image for
a tired executive chair.

A 12-year-old executive office chair in beige wool, worn through to the foam on the right arm, is hardly the stuff of dreams. But after being treated to a new tea cup front and a midnight blue back, embellished with embroidery, it has leapt into the realms of fantasy.

With only three yards of the print at my disposal there were limits to its distribution so I settled for plain outside arms, outside back and under-side of seat. As the fabrics were rather light in weight for upholstery, they were bonded to fusible wadding for more heft. And because the print has a light background, removable antimacassars were made for the head rest and arms and the finished chair was sprayed with a dirt repellent preparation.

The hand-embroidered tea cup hints at the richness of the past when chairs were adorned with fine needlework, often in silver and gold threads. However, this rendition is strictly modern. The cut-out motif was bonded to the outside back fabric with paper-backed fusible web. With a needle threaded with four strands of embroidery cotton, the diamond-shaped segments of the pattern were quickly covered in satin stitch.

Office chairs like this seem to have many different kinds of screws and bolts to hold their various parts together. To avoid confusion when reconstructing the chair, store them in well labelled, self-sealing plastic bags.

All the old upholstery fabric was saved, seams were unpicked and the pieces used for patterns. Even the black cambric fly strips which shaped the pull-ins or indents on the inside back were re-used, as were the bulk-reducing cambric extensions from the back and seat covers. It was also easier to use the old Velcro® because it was exactly the right size.

Stripping Old Upholstery

With screwdriver, prise off outside arms; these had corner-fixed ridged plastic plugs which clipped into cavities in the outer face of the moulded plastic inside arms.

Turn chair over and, with appropriate tool (Allen key in this instance), undo fastenings on central pedestal. Place pedestal hardware in self-sealing plastic bags and label. Store all removed hardware in this manner throughout the disassembling of the chair.

1 Hardboard outside arms with ridged plastic plugs.

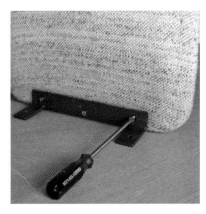

2 Unscrewing brackets from inside arms.

3 Moulded plastic inside arm prior to stripping.

4 Seat cover after removal showing black canvas extension.

5 Releasing the back cover (extension flap removed).

6 Foam liner folded back to reveal fly strip at first indent.

7 Another fly strip is revealed, first one has been released.

8 Inside out old cover. Note labelled foam blocks.

On underside of seat, use screwdriver to remove staples securing the black cambric platform cloth. Reserve cloth.

Release screws on metal brackets attaching inside arms to underside of seat and screws through inside arms to sides of chair. Unscrew metal bracket from inside arm.

Prise away staples on all arm pieces, label old upholstery and press flat for patterns.

The shape is moulded plywood in two pieces (back and seat) supported by an iron frame. Using screwdriver, remove staples from the underside which attach the fabric from the outside back, inside back and seat. At this stage, the order of work is revealed. Remove seat fabric and unpick seams and Velcro®. Label (use white marker on black cambric fly strip) and press pieces.

Pull the end of the inside back through seat crevice to the front; the inside back fabric had been stitched to a foam liner. Unpick and label extension strip then start unpicking the side seams – these had been slipstitched up to the first indent. Glue had also been used which proved troublesome to dislodge; the foam became pitted in places by its removal.

At the first indent, the fly strip was stapled into the plywood beneath a slit in the foam padding of the inside back. Remove staples from fly strip and continue to roll cover and its liner upwards to next fly strip. With black marker, label abutting edges of foam in centre section of inside back.

When back cover is released, unpick side seams and horizontal stitching holding foam and fly strips in place. Label and press all fabric pieces. Reserve foam.

Unzip separate seat cushion. Foam was in two parts, divided by a zippered chamber. Label front and back pieces. Cushion padding segments are made from a core of firm foam with a top wrap of soft foam. Unpick seam, zips and Velcro® and reserve.

Embroidering the Cup

Drape fabric for outside back over the outside back of chair to determine central placement of the embroidered motif and mark position with pins. Select a motif from the fabric and cut it out so it is centred in a square. Cut fusible web the same size and, following manufacturer's instructions, bond to back of motif. Cut around motif as accurately as possible and bond it to designated position on outside back of fabric.

Place motif in embroidery hoop and, using four strands of embroidery thread, fill in the diamond-shaped segments with satin stitch, changing needles when necessary. Here, stitches were placed horizontally on the cup and angled down on the saucer so they would enhance the design. Rim of the cup and outline of the saucer were worked in stem stitch.

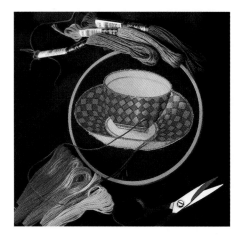

9 Threads were selected to match tea cup colors exactly.

10 Satin stitched cup with stem-stitched outlines.

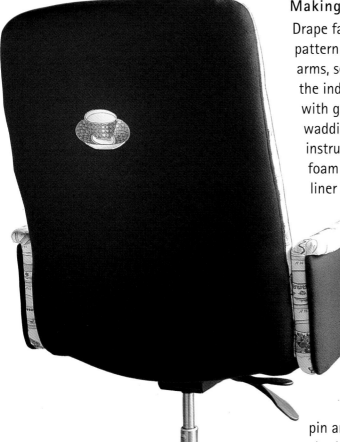

Back view of chair.

Making the Inside Back Cover

Drape fabric over the inside back and decide on pattern placement for inside back as well as inside arms, seat and separate seat cushion. Because of the indents in the foam liner, cut the inside back with generous seam allowances. Bond fusible wadding to the fabric following manufacturer's instructions and place the bonded fabric over the foam liner, ensuring that the raised side of the liner is against the fused wadding and that centres are aligned.

Starting from the centre, pin through the layers working out in all directions in a sunburst pattern; to top and bottom, side to side, diagonally to all four hypothetical corners and once in between all these lines.

Then tack on these pinned lines, again working from the centre out. Place fly strips on back of foam liner, pin and tack in place before top stitching over the horizontal stitching lines in the grooves of the liner.

In the outer seam allowance sew liner and inside back fabric together. Snip and release all tacking threads.

Joining the Back Cover

Cut outside back to size using original piece as a pattern, and bond the wrong side of outside back to fusible wadding following manufacturer's instructions.

With right sides together, pin outside back to inside back. Refer to original pieces; the inside back upper corners were eased with tiny gathers to give fullness which accommodated the front foam padding. Repeat this easing, tack around outside edge and check the fit of the corners on the chair with cover inside out.

Stitch from first indent on lower side, around top to same place on other side. Snip and release tacking. Clip seams at corners, turn to right side, press and, with sewing threads to match fabrics, top stitch 5 mm (¼ in) from seam line on both sides.

Stitch extension strip to bottom raw edge of inside back.

11 Cutting outside back fabric from original cover piece.

12 After pinning and tacking, inside front is machine stitched.

13 Seat cover with eased corners is tacked prior to machine stitching.

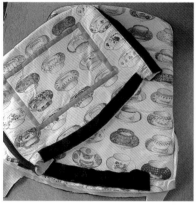

14 Velcro® topped seat and back ready to be stapled.

15 Rear foam is inserted through zip opening of the separate cushion.

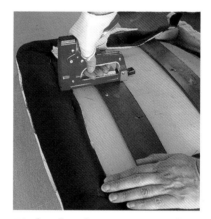

16 Stapling the seat cover to the plywood base.

17 With corners aligned, back cover is pulled on.

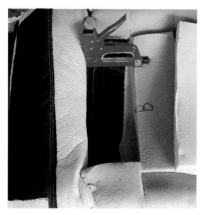

18 Stapling a fly strip in place to make an indent.

19 Slip stitching the side opening of the back cover closed.

Making the Seat Cover

Using original upholstery pieces as patterns, cut fabrics for underside of seat and top of seat and bond their wrong sides to fusible wadding. Note easing on corners of underside seat and, when pinning both pieces with right sides together, repeat this with tiny gathers. Tack outside seam and check fit on chair with cover inside out. Stitch seam, clip corners, snip and release tacking thread and turn through to right side. Press and top stitch on both sides of seam line as for back cover.

Stitch extension strip to raw edge of top of seat and stitch Velcro® rectangle in place, copying its exact position from old cover.

Making the Cushion

Cut top and bottom cushion pieces from print fabric and fusible wadding using the original cover for a pattern. Fuse wadding to wrong side of fabric following manufacturer's instructions. Mark position of Velcro® rectangle on cushion bottom and top stitch in place. Then mark position of the double-ended zipper which makes the chamber between the two foam inserts on the inside of the top and bottom. Stitch both sides of zip in place, stitching very close to the outer edge of the zip. Stitch the other zipper into the back of the cushion bottom. With right sides together, join top and bottom around outside edge and turn to right side through zipper opening. Press and top stitch on both sides of seam line around cushion edge as for back cover. Insert first piece of foam into the front of cushion with soft foam wrap on top. Close off zipper chamber then insert rear foam piece (soft side up). Close outside zipper.

Stapling Down the Cover

Position the seat cover on the seat, poke extension flap through seat crevice and turn chair over. On the underside of seat, start to staple at the centre front, then pull on extension flap and fix it with a staple at centre. Staple at opposite centres of the sides and move out to the corners, gathering excess and pleating before stapling to accommodate corner padding.

Making sure all blocks of cut foam are in their right slots on the inside back and, with the back cover inside out, start to ease it onto the chair. Make sure corners are correctly positioned and the sides are firmly pulled down before stapling first fly strip to the plywood of the inside back. Pulling firmly on fly strip, staple in the centre first then work out to both sides. Staple all fly strips and then slip stitch the opening below the first indent closed, using a curved needle and invisible nylon thread.

With marker, or pins, mark positions for screws from the arms.

Poke extension flap from inside back down through the seat crevice and turn the chair over. Starting from the centre and working out, staple extension flap of inside back to underside of seat, pulling firmly to exert pressure on the fabric and eliminate wrinkles.

Then pull down the raw edges of the outside back and staple to the underside of seat, starting from the centre and working out.

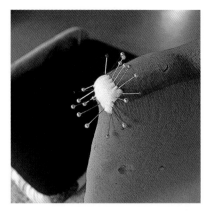

20 Mending the front of the right arm rest with glued foam.

21 Stapling fabric to one of the inside arm pieces.

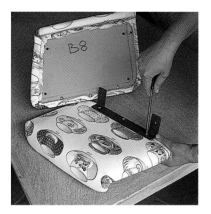

22 Screwing bracket to lower edge of inside arm.

23 Bracket from inside arm screwed to underside of seat.

24 Top antimacassar was pattern matched to cover and scalloped.

The Arms

The front of the right arm rest was worn through to the plastic so it was padded with a little polyester fibrefill (white toy filling) and then patched with a small rectangle of foam which was glued into position and pinned until dry.

Using the old covers as patterns, fabric for the arm pieces was cut and fused to the wadding. One corner of the hardboard outside arm was almost cracked through but I was able to stabilise the split with staples and fasten the fabric further towards the centre. Stapling into hardboard and plastic posed no problems. Fabric was stretched taut between staples on opposite sides; the corners were neatly pleated to take up the excess. Holes for screws were noted and marked on inside arms.

Holes were poked through with a stitch ripper for screws in the arms and sides and brackets were screwed to the inside arms. Inside arms were screwed through to the sides and the brackets were screwed to the underside of seat.

Reserved black cambric platform cloth was stapled over the underside to hide any raw edges and the pedestal was repositioned and fixed in place.

Outside arms were clipped on and pushed into place.

Calico-backed antimacassars were made for the arms and head rest. They were all pattern matched to their respective covers and the head rest was scalloped around the saucer bottoms.

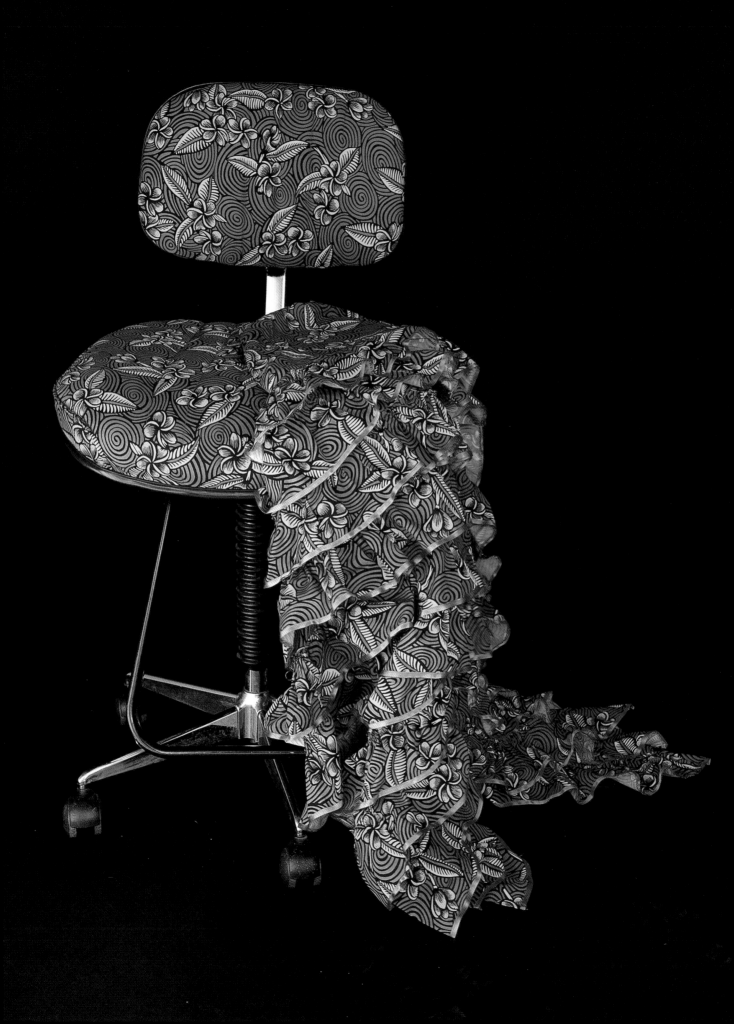

CHAIR with DETACHABLE SKIRT

MATERIALS

Phillips head screwdriver

Screwdriver

Stitch ripper

Scissors

Sufficient fabric
(see text at right)

Matching thread

Staple gun

19.2 m (21 yd) of 6 mm
(¼ in) wide satin ribbon

Marking pencil

2.5 m (2¾ yd) of
narrow cord

Formerly indistinguishable from many thousands of others which were produced about 15 years ago, this battery-bred drafting chair has undergone a dramatic metamorphosis. Weary of its regulation green woolen upholstery, I decided it needed a new personality. A day later the chair emerged with a flurry of frills; an exotic hothouse hybrid clothed in colour, pattern and cut suited only to the most advanced workplace – my office at home. Why a skirt? If a Victorian piano can have a shawl, surely an ordinary office chair can have a frilly skirt. The original idea was to use the skirt to hide the chair's footrest which looked to me like a stray prosthesis. Although designed specifically to go around the chair, I prefer the skirt draped over the seat, like a matador's cape.

Re-upholstering the seat and back will take as little as 60 cm or ⅔ yd. By cutting the width of the skirt parallel with the selvedge (railroading), the chair and skirt can be cut out of 3.2 m (3½ yd) of 152 cm (60 in) wide fabric.

Although they may appear to be impenetrable, you can get to the inner workings of these chairs. At the outside back of this one, there is a fitting which can be undone with a Phillips head screwdriver and this releases the back. By inserting a couple of screwdrivers as levers into the groove between the outside back and inside back, the two pieces which are both molded plastic, pop apart.

The pedestal is attached to the plywood seat support with coach screws which can be removed with a socket or box spanner. However, I left it fixed and worked with the pedestal attached.

Back

With the inside back free, prise away the staples fastening the upholstery fabric to the plastic with a screwdriver. Here, the fabric was attached to a foam liner by five rows of stitching; release stitching with a stitch ripper.

From the original back cover, cut a new back with generous seam allowance all around. Place wrong side of fabric over the raised side of the liner, aligning centres of both pieces. Starting at the centre, pin fabric to the foam in the groove made by the previous stitching. Pin fabric to remaining indents, working from the centre out. Machine stitch along the pinned lines.

Place fabric over inside back support. Ensuring it is centred, turn over and staple to its back, working first from centres of all sides and moving out to the rounded corners.

Snap the inside back onto the outside back.

Seat

Fabric was fastened to the edge of the plywood of the seat. This row of staples had been covered by a flexible plastic strip which, in section, looks like a squashed 'S'. The upper 'lip' of the 'S' enclosed the tops of the staples

Chair with skirt draped on seat.

Top of plastic strip folds
down to cover staples.

that held the strip to the edge of the plywood; the lower part gripped the underside edge of the seat. Both rows of staples were removed with a screwdriver and the strip reserved. As for the back, the seat fabric was attached to a foam liner by five rows of stitching.

Stitching at the piped edge of the boxing strip was unpicked with a stitch ripper. Piping, which was plastic tubing, was cut away from its fabric enclosure. Stitching of channelling on seat was also unpicked.

Original seat and boxing strip fabric pieces were pressed and used as patterns.

Cut a new seat with generous seams all around to allow for channelled stitching. Cut new boxing strip the same size as the old. For the piping, cut a strip on the straight grain of fabric; the old one was cut this way as a precaution against stretching.

Following the placement and sequence for the back, stitch the seat in channels to the foam liner. Trim sides and back seam allowances level with the edge of the foam liner. Fold piping strip of fabric in half lengthwise over the plastic tube (right side out) and with raw edges matching and a zipper foot, stitch as close as possible to the tube. With raw edges matching, sew piping to sides and back of seat, following the previous 'trail' of the tapered line down to the lower front outside edges of seat. Starting from the centre back and working out in both directions, pin boxing strip to seat fabric, right sides together and all raw edges matching. Then stitch boxing strip to seat.

Matching centre backs and centre fronts on both the seat of the chair and the upholstery assembly, staple through right side of fabric to the outside edge of the plywood seat support. Match centre front of seat with centre front of plastic edging strip, ensure its bottom lip encloses the lower edge of the plywood and staple through the centre of the strip. Work out in both directions and finish at the centre back.

Skirt

Cut a piece of fabric 48 cm x 195 cm (19 in x 2 yd 5 in) for the skirt. Narrow hem two short and one long side.

From the width of the fabric cut 12 strips each 9.5 cm (3¾ in) deep. Machine zigzag around edges of strips to prevent fraying. Then 6 mm (¼ in) from the edge, sew short ends of two strips, right sides together, raw edges matching. Repeat for remaining ten strips, making six joined strips in all.

Top stitch ribbon to one long side of each joined strip with wrong side of ribbon lapped over the right side of fabric. Gather the other long side on the sewing machine.

Skirt held by cord tied
around top of plastic strip.

Lay the top edge of one frill over the skirt's lower edge with wrong side of frill over right side of skirt. With pins, attach the frills to the skirt starting at the lower edge, aligning centre of frill and centre of skirt, adjusting gathers evenly. Top stitch 6 mm (¼ in) from top of frill.

Lay the next frill 8 cm (3⅛ in) above the top of the first and stitch down in the same way. Continue until all frills are stitched to skirt.

To enclose and hide the raw edge of the top frill, fold top of skirt down over top frill, right sides together, and stitch 1 cm (⅜ in) from the fold. Open and press.

Finishing

Check skirt length on chair. Mark a line for the casing for the cord. Then turn down and stitch a 12 mm (½ in) casing. Thread cord through casing at top of skirt.

Replace the fitting on the outside back of the chair and arrange skirt around the top of the plastic strip of seat and tie firmly at the back of seat.

ACKNOWLEDGEMENTS

Many people helped in many ways in the production of this book and, in particular, I would like to thank Trisha Malcolm for her labour and inspiration in the closing moments of the project. Her keen observation that 'one side always turns out better than the other' could well serve as the amateur upholsterer's motto. My sister, Annette Wallis, who pioneers problem solving in the domestic and craft arenas with acute intelligence honed by scientific training, was frequently a very welcome extra pair of hands. Sincere thanks are also due to Jenny Cattell, the editor, and to those in the magazine, publishing, design, decorating and fabric worlds, including Stephanie King, Wendy Roberts, James Marks, Anna Heywood, Stewart Merrett, Helen Kiel, Georgina Weir, Sally Milner and Patti Tonkin.

DESIGN, FABRIC AND SUPPLIER ACKNOWLEDGEMENTS

Page 10, Designers Guild fabric, Wardlaw, Sydney.
Page 13, Liberty fabric.
Page 14, Rowe Fabrics, Sydney.
Page 15, Seapines fabric, Rowe Fabrics, Sydney.
Pages 18-21, Designer: Rae Ganim, Melbourne.
Page 25, Designers: Sophie Blackall and Nick Godlee, Sydney.
Page 26 top, Rowe Fabrics, Sydney.
Page 30, Designers Guild fabric.
Page 34 above, Designers Guild fabric, Wardlaw, Sydney.
Page 36 right, H.A. Percheron fabric.
Page 37, Laura Ashley fabric.
Pages 40, 42, 43, Bryan Yates Upholstery, Sydney.
Pages 41, 45, 50, John Puddick Furnishings, Sydney.
Page 54, Sahco Hesslein of Germany fabrics from South Pacific Fabrics, Sydney.
Page 55, Rowe Fabrics, Sydney.
Page 60, Rowe Fabrics, Sydney.
Page 61, Fabrics and trimmings from Thomas Dare, London.
Page 79, Laura Ashley fabric.
Page 83, Designers Guild fabric, Wardlaw, Sydney.
Page 107, Inside back and outside back, Souvenir d'Afrique from Warner; right inside arm and left outside arm, Safi from Osborne & Little, left inside arm and right outside arm, Merlin from Osborne & Little; boxing strips on cushions and arm and back borders, a Liberty cotton, Cottage Garden from the Chiltern Collection; seat front and platform top, Pierre Frey 1898 Barbizon Outremer 76; cushion tops, Montbrison from Designers Guild. All from Wardlaw, Sydney.
Pages 126, 128, 129, Bush Babies from Rowe Fabrics, Sydney.
Page 131, Designer, Vicki Calligeros, Sydney.
Page 139, Designer, Sophie Blackall, Sydney.
Page 147, 151, Designers Guild fabrics made by Stitches Soft Furnishings, Sydney.
Pages 154, 158, Nobilis fabrics from Redelman Fabrics, Sydney, made by John Puddick Furnishings, Sydney.
Page 161, Minton by Pierre Frey from Wardlaw, Sydney.
Page 168, Frangipanni by Mambo, Sydney.

PHOTOGRAPHIC ACKNOWLEDGEMENTS

Photography by Simon Blackall, with the exception of the following:
Pages 6-7, Henry Bourne, Options, Robert Harding Syndication.
Page 9, Chris Drake, Country Homes & Interiors, Robert Harding Syndication.
Page 26 above, Rodney Weidland, Australian House & Garden.
Page 27, Hugh Johnson, Homes & Gardens, Robert Harding Syndication.
Page 28, Rodney Weidland, Australian House & Garden.
Pages 28-29, Kiloran Howard, Homes & Gardens, Robert Harding Syndication.
Page 30, J. Merrell, Homes & Gardens, Robert Harding Syndication.
Page 31 right, Polly Wreford, Homes & Gardens, Robert Harding Syndication.
Pages 32-33, Polly Wreford, Homes & Gardens, Robert Harding Syndication.
Page 34 right, Jan Baldwin, Homes & Gardens, Robert Harding Syndication.
Page 35, Jan Baldwin, Homes & Gardens, Robert Harding Syndication.
Page 36 right, David Barrett, Homes & Gardens, Robert Harding Syndication.
Page 36 below, Rodney Weidland, Australian House & Garden.
Page 38 right, Trevor Richards, Homes & Gardens, Robert Harding Syndication.
Page 38 below, Rodney Weidland, Australian House & Garden.
Page 39 right, Rodney Weidland, Australian House & Garden.
Pages 40-45, 50, 54, Andrew Payne, Photographix.
Pages 83-86, Russell Brooks, Australian House & Garden.
Pages 147, 150, 154, 158, Tandy Rowley, Belle Design and Decoration.

GLOSSARY

Back tacking strips: purchased or homemade slim cardboard strips used in back tacking.

Back tacking: a method of attaching two pieces of fabric (right sides together, raw edges matching) to a chair frame beneath a slender strip of cardboard (back tacking strip) with tacks or staples. The cardboard strip gives a neat edge to the seam when opened out, and also evenly distributes the grip of the staples or tacks in the timber along fabric 'seam'.

Baste: to stitch temporarily, either by hand or machine using large stitches, before stitching permanently. Permanent stitching is usually done towards the raw edge side of the basting so basting can be easily unpicked. Many modern sewing machines can be set to baste.

Box spanner: tubular tool which fits over a nut or the hexagonal head of a bolt, and is turned from above by means of a rod (tommy bar) passed through a pair of holes in the upper part of the tube.

Calico: a firm, plain-weave unbleached or white cotton fabric. Originally a printed cotton fabric imported from India and later manufactured in the West. In the USA, calico is a strong printed cotton.

Casing: an open-ended hem, usually at the top of curtains, where the curtain rod is inserted.

Chaise longue: a type of chair used for reclining, with a padded back rest and the seat extended to form a leg rest.

Channelling: a ribbed effect achieved by enclosing stuffing in fabric tunnels.

Chintz: fine cotton fabric, usually glazed or semi-glazed, frequently printed with brightly colored designs.

Chipboard: see particle board.

Cupola: a small dome which forms a decorative element on a roof.

Dowel: round rod in various sizes, ranging from 3 - 55 mm ($\frac{1}{8}$ - $2\frac{1}{4}$ in) in hardwood or softwood, widely used for making strong joins in timber.

Edge roll: a firm and rounded profile in stuffing brought out beyond the line of the chair frame and held in place by stitching through hessian (burlap) undercover with twine and an upholstery needle. Flanged ready-made edge roll of compressed paper can be purchased by length.

Extension flap: inexpensive fabric sewn to the edge of cover fabric and used as an economy measure. The extension flap is hidden from view once a piece of furniture is upholstered.

Finger press: where using an iron would be awkward, you can exert pressure with the fingers on a proposed seam line in order to make a crease.

Fly piece: as for extension flap, but also a strip of fabric which is sewn to the wrong side of the cover fabric (usually for the inside back) and used to drag the cover into slits in the stuffing or foam.

Furbelow: an excessive trimming, usually of pleated or gathered fabric. Originally a term associated with women's gowns.

Fusible web: mostly sold with a peel-away paper backing, these non-woven adhesive fibres are sensitive to heat and are used to bond two layers of fabric together.

Grain: in woven fabric, the grain is the direction, either horizontal or vertical, in which the threads run.

Grosgrain ribbon: usually a rayon ribbon with the weft (cross) threads much larger than the warp (lengthwise threads) resulting in a horizontally ribbed effect.

Gusset: an extra piece of fabric inserted in a seam to allow movement or to accommodate a change in plane.

Hardboard: cabinet making and internal sheet building material made from heat- and pressure-treated wood fibres, usually with one smooth side and the other with a wire mesh texture.

Hessian (burlap US): made from jute, this coarse, plain-weave fabric comes in various weights and is used for sacks and carpet backing, as well as for covering webbing, springs and stuffing in upholstery.

Ikat: fabrics patterned with distinctive fuzzy motifs in simple shapes as a result of dyeing tied bundles of yarn prior to the weaving process. Developed in Indonesia.

Jute: strong fibre from the inner bark of two East Indian plants — used for making hessian, twine and rope.

MDF: an abbreviation for medium-density fibreboard, which is a highly compressed general purpose building board made from wood fibres and resins. It ranges in thickness from 3 - 32 mm ($\frac{1}{8}$ - $1\frac{1}{8}$ in), and is a very stable material which does not splinter when cut or sawn.

Mitre, mitring: to cut two identical pieces (fabric, timber etc) at a 45° degree angle in order to join them to make a 90° angle.

Moiré: a fabric with a wavy watermarked appearance which is produced either during the weaving process, or as a result of the finished fabric being pressed between two cylinders.

Muslin: cotton gauze-like lining fabric for lightweight

fabrics. In the USA, muslin is what is known in the UK and Australia as calico.

Nap: pile on fabrics such as velours and velvets, or a finish raised by combing or with abrasive rollers which lies in one direction only.

Ottoman: a low upholstered footstool which originated in Turkey and was adopted by the West in the late 18th century.

Over-stuffed: upholstery padding built out beyond the timber framework of a piece of furniture.

Overlocker: a multi-threaded sewing machine which stitches, trims and overcasts the seam at the same time.

Palanquin: a covered and curtained box-like seat or bed supported by shafts, carried on the shoulders of four or more men.

Particle board: factory-made board, consisting of wood particles and resins bonded together under pressure and heat.

Pelmet: draped fabric or a more solid three-sided projection above a window or door to conceal the runners or rings of curtains or blinds.

Piece, pieced: fabric required for frills, skirts and the inside and outside backs of large sofas is frequently far in excess of the width of the fabric, so it is necessary to join or piece together sufficient widths to achieve the span.

Placket: an opening left along a seam for closure with zippers, buttons or ties.

Polyester fibrefill: most commonly used as a pillow filling and sold as toy filling in small quantities, this material is teased out and used as upholstery stuffing.

Polyester wadding: white fleecy-layered padding made from strong, resilient, chemically produced fibres. Available in various thicknesses and widths, it is sold by the metre (or yard) from a roll and used as a levelling and softening layer beneath upholstery fabric.

Post: the upright members (usually timber) of a chair frame.

Puddle: to cut lengths of fabric (usually curtains) longer than necessary so it they 'spill' onto the floor instead of just touching or clearing it.

Raffia: the dried fibre taken from the leaf stalks of a Madagascan palm.

Rail: the horizontal members (usually timber) of a chair frame.

Railroading: using fabric sideways to avoid joins in the backs and seats of sofas.

Rattail: a thin silk untwisted cord.

Selvedge (selvage): the two outer edges of a length of woven fabric are usually more tightly woven, like tape, for strength and to avoid fraying. Selvedges are cut away before fabric pieces are sewn together.

Serger: see overlocker.

Shirred: fabric gathered between two threads or drawstrings.

Slipcover: covers additional to upholstery which can be removed and laundered. Originally used during summer and therefore made from fabrics such as linen or cotton which are cool to touch.

Slip stitch: can be invisible if worked carefully and is sewn by hand to close a seam from the right side. Start just inside one of the folds and working from right to left and side to side, make tiny stitches, pulling thread tight enough to join but not wrinkle folds.

Slip tack: a temporary fixing made by driving a tack halfway into a surface. Slip tacks are not re-useable and, once removed, are discarded.

Socket spanner: used like a box spanner for loosening and tightening nuts in awkward spaces. Some have ratchet handles and jointed extensions.

Spoon back: refers to the spoon-like shape of the back of a dining chair with upholstered seat and back.

Tack: (sewing), see baste.

Ticking: traditional white or natural cotton twill fabric with black woven stripes for mattress and pillow covers, now available in other coloured stripes.

Top stitch: hand or machine stitching on the right side of the fabric used as a decorative accent and to secure edges or seams.

Twill: a common weave with the weft threads woven under two and over two of the warp threads in one row and offset over and under two different threads in the next. As a result, a diagonal pattern appears in the threads of the fabric.

Warp: threads fixed lengthwise on a loom which will run parallel to the selvedges of the fabric.

Weft: threads interlaced across the warp during the weaving process which are at right angles to the selvedges.

White glue: quick- and clear-drying general household adhesive intended for interior woodworking repairs, which will also stick fabric to fabric and fabric to timber.

BIBLIOGRAPHY

Collins Complete Book of Soft Furnishings. HarperCollins Publishers, London, 1993.

FASTNEDGE, RALPH. English Furniture Styles 1500–1830. Penguin Books, Middlesex, England. First published 1955. Reprinted 1961, 1962, 1964, 1967, 1969, 1979.

GRIMES, KITTY (ed). The Illustrated Guide to Furniture Repair and Restoration. Marshall Cavendish Books, London and Arco Publishing, New York, 1980.

HIRSCHMAN, JESSICA ELIN. For Your Home, Upholstery. Friedman Group, New York, 1993.

JAMES, DAVID. Upholstery Techniques and Projects. Guild of Master Craftsman Publications, Lewes, East Sussex, England, 1994.

JOHNSTONE, JAMES B. and the Sunset Editorial Staff. Furniture Upholstery and Repair. Lane Books, Menlo Park, California, 1970. Eighth printing, 1974.

JOY, EDWARD T. The Country Life Library of Antiques, Chairs. Country Life Books, London, 1967, 1968, revised edition 1980.

JOY, EDWARD. The Connoisseur Illustrated Guides, Furniture. The Connoisseur, London, 1972.

LEBEAU, CAROLINE. Fabrics, The Decorative Art of Textiles. Thames and Hudson, London, 1994.

LUKE, HEATHER. Upholstery. Weldon Russell, North Sydney, in association with Rosemary Wilkinson, 1993.

STEPHENSON, JOHN W. Modern Furniture Upholstering, A Practical Handbook for the Upholsterer. Clifford and Lawton, New York, 1923. Reprinted by Potterton Books, England.

INDEX